GOT IT GOIN' ON - II

POWER TOOLS FOR GIRLS!

BY JANICE FEREBEE, MSW

Revised Edition

Celebrating Over 20 Years Empowering Girls

Contributors

Dr. Glenda Clare, Behavioral Health Care Management Consultant

DIPLOMACY

"Sticks and stones may break bones, but words can cut to the core. Words are more powerful than we realize. Mere words can convince a child that she or he is worthless and unloved."

--March 28 Entry from Black Pearls by ERIC V. COPAGE
®1995 BY ERIC COPAGE
Reprinted with permission of HarperCollins Publishing, Inc.
WILLIAM MORROW

(Symbol of the perpetual existence of man's spirit)

"Speak LIFE to our children . . .
for they become what you tell them!"
— Janice Ferebee, MSW

Library of Congress Control Number: 00-132336
ISBN: 978-0-9651166-3-3

Got It Goin' On-II
POWER TOOLS FOR GIRLS! Revised Edition
Copyright © 2022 by Janice Ferebee

For permission requests, please contact the author via the "Contact" page at
* www.authorjaniceferebee.com

Angel Illustrations by Candice Bradley * www.bycandicebradley.com

Cover Design by Moneeka Gentry-Stanifer & Mosi Design

Proudly Self-published by Divine Legacy Publishing * www.divinelegacypublishing.com

Graphic Design & Layout by Created by Moneeka * www.createdbymoneeka.com

Adinkra Symbols from The Adinkra Dictionary by W. BRUCE WILLIS ©1998, by W. BRUCE WILLIS Reprinted with permission of The Pyramid Complex

In memory of my family – my mother and father,

Elliot & Elizabeth Ferebee, and my sisters Denise and Annette (all deceased) –where GIRL POWER was appreciated and nurtured.

I miss you all.

Rest in Eternal Peace & Power

Other Works by Janice Ferebee, MSW

Got It Goin' On: An Image Awareness Guide for Young Ladies

Got It Goin' On-II: Facilitator's Guide * Revised Edition

Praise for Got It Goin' On-II: Revised Edition

"To say I am proud of you would truly be an understatement. This is a must-read handbook that needs to be in the hand of every girl. Thank you for your enduring commitment and trailblazing work to empower our girls. This is a movement."
- Erica Austin | Author, Motivational Speaker & Youth Advocate

"Janice Ferebee's work and commitment to our nation's girls is unparalleled."
- Sophia Nelson | Award-Winning Author & Journalist

"As Black & Brown girls face increased racism and discrimination, Janice Ferebee (my Alpha Kappa Alpha Soror) offers girls a timely, culturally competent revised edition of her popular GOT IT GOIN' ON-II personal development handbook. Her use of the GOT IT GOIN' ON® GUARDIAN ANGELS is an imaginative way to help girls courageously navigate adolescence. As the mother of two grown daughters, I encourage all parents to purchase this effective empowerment tool today! It's a MUST HAVE for every Black and Brown girl's personal library as she evolves into womanhood."
- Vanessa Bell Calloway | Actress, Director, Producer, Wife, Mother, and Lover of Life!

"I met Janice at SEVENTEEN Magazine at the time she was the magazine's first African American Models Editor, and I was their first Latina intern. Janice has been working for over 40 years since then to help Black & Brown girls deal with our trauma, our issues, and our circumstances, to find our voices and our deserved place and seat at any table and in any career."
- Nely Galan | Former President of TV Network Telemundo & NY Times Best Selling Author of SELF MADE: Becoming Empowered, Self-Reliant, and Rich in Every Way | 2016, Random House

My Gratitude Speaks...

Well, here we are again – two decades (20+ years) from the release of the first edition of this handbook, GIGO-II. I can hardly contain my gratitude for all those who helped me complete the updates and revisions to this revised edition.

First, I give ultimate praise and honor to GOD for continuing to guide me through this project and for revealing my life's purpose. My family and friends continue to bless me with their support and encouragement: The memories of my mother and father, Elizabeth and Elliot Ferebee (deceased), and my sisters, Denise and Annette (deceased); other female family members – Christine G.Y., Pam, Kyna, Madeline, Christine B., Akira, Alexis, Jordan, Trenise, and Trinity; and the fellas – Carey Charles, Tramaine, Traquez, Triston, Kwame, Kofi, Cousin Hal (deceased), and Uncle Victor -- who have purchased books or spread the word. I love and thank you all.

Thank you to my close friends and new collaborators – many who have been on this journey since the first book, my programs, graduate school, my cancer journeys, election to public office, and now – the *GOT IT GOIN' ON-II: REVISED EDITION!* Thanks for continuing to believe in me. Here's to you – Carolyn B.P., Carolyn F.N., Darrell, Delphine (deceased), Denise, Donna, Doreen, Eddie, Jacquie, Janice, Karyn, Lenny, Mae, Michele, Robin, Ruth, Sophia, Tara, Teddy, Tuere, Weyman (deceased), Warren, Warren, and . . .

What an honor for my work and me to be recognized by The Oprah Winfrey Show and ESSENCE Magazine! The Got It Goin' On® (GIGO) Foundation and Empowerment Program for Girls (based on the original GIGO-II handbook) were featured on The Oprah Winfrey Show in 2001. I was also recognized by ESSENCE Magazine with their 2003 "Street Warrior" ESSENCE Award.

Special acknowledgement to all the newspapers, radio and television stations, bookstores, individuals, organizations, and social media outlets over time that have promoted my projects. Special acknowledgment to Black bookstores across the country who carried my books (many out-of-business now); Jacquie Gales Webb, Darlene Jackson, Tony Richards, Triscena Gray, and Rene Nash of WHUR, Washington, D.C; and Denise Rolark Barnes of the Washington Informer. Thanks for promoting my important female empowerment message.

There aren't enough words to thank all the girls who read my first book and participated in my empowerment work-shops . . . you are all the reason that I labor in the field! Because you shared your lives and concerns, I have been able to make updates that incorporate the new information and challenges affecting your lives today. Special thanks to girls from the DC Metropolitan Police Department's Youth Outreach Program and Maryland Girl Scout Troop members – Kennadi, Ziyah, Tyler, and Mykah. I pray it will make a difference in your lives. And to the GIGO alumnae, I am forever grateful to you for allowing me to pour into your lives over the last 20 years. I will not be able to name you all but know that you are all in my heart. I am looking forward to great things from you all – Ashley, Chavery, Danielle, Ebony, Jessica, Latasha, Lauren, Malinda, Mykayla, Ryanne, Savannah, Shayla, Sumiya, Symone, Taylor . . .

Special gratitude to the adults who became part of the GIGO family who made this dream work -- Adjoa, Angelique, Elethia (my right hand), Jasmine, Kenisha, Michelle, Rose and Eleanor from Roosevelt, NY, Roxanne, Ora, Tene, Tineal (my mentee, assistant, and Soror), and Todd.

Thank you Kenneth Smith, for your amazing curriculum design and development of the Got It Goin' On-II: Facilitator's Guide (released in 2005), and Dr. Glenda Clare for taking on the updated version scheduled for release in 2022. In addition, my eternal gratitude to Rodney Jackson who pushed me to be true to my passion.

I also want to express my gratitude to Rodney Herring for updating his original cover designs with the creative finishing touches by Moneeka Gentry Stanifer and Candice Bradley for reimagining the GIGO Guardian Angels - GRACE, JOY, FAITH, LOVE, HOPE, PEACE, & CHARITY. I LOVE these new images! Special thanks to Moneeka Gentry Stanifer for her creative layout and design. And thanks to Amanda Chambers and Divine Legacy Publishing for pulling it all together - editing, branding, and social media coaching; and Martin Pratt for his insightful marketing and promotional direction.

Finally, these generous individuals made it possible to go the last mile to get this handbook off to the printer - Carolyne, Hosiah, Marcia, Richard, Marian, Deborah, Diane, Doris, Desi, Mary, Janice, Judy, Gregory, Natalie, Candice, Robin, Alexandra, LaFern, Darlene, and Ora. Bless you all!

I am eternally grateful for all of the support I received to complete the revised edition, no matter how big or small the task - I LOVE AND THANK YOU ALL!

YOU HAVE BEEN THE WIND BENEATH MY WINGS!

Janice Ferebee, MSW

Author

GOT IT GOIN' ON - II

POWER TOOLS FOR GIRLS!
Revised Edition

"Standards of Excellence"

Introduction

"We have the power to create a new way of being that the world has not yet known if we enter this new era with faith, courage and a loving agenda. We can rise up and become who God intends us to be. In this new era, let us be in peace."

(from In The Spirit-1/2000)

-- Susan L. Taylor

Founder - National CARES Mentoring

Editor-in-Chief Emeritus-ESSENCE Magazine

I am glad you opened this book. My prayer is that something you read will make a difference in your life. Girls are one of the world's most precious natural treasures. Many people have forgotten that, and it is time we reminded them. This personal development handbook and social-emotional learning tool is my gift to you, to honor your presence and to remind you that there are many people who care about you.

Girls often face increasing challenges which threaten to derail their futures – challenges such as boredom, loneliness (especially during COVID-19), parental absence and neglect, mental/physical/sexual abuse, stress, depression, suicide, violence, bullying, gangs, trafficking, abusive cultural practices, early sexual exposure and activity, teenage pregnancy, HIV/AIDS and STDs, low academic achievement, low expectations, lack of access to quality education, lack of knowledge of girls' rights, poor self-image, media exploitation, destructive social media behavior, "reality show" nonsense, lack of cultural pride, and lack of spiritual guidance and positive role models. Every girl deserves a happy, healthy, and whole future. I wrote this book to enable more girls to experience the joys of being a girl and to help transition them into caring, confident, culturally, mentally, socially, and spiritually competent young ladies. It is my prayer that Got It Goin' On-II will improve the quality of life for every girl who reads it.

Many issues that challenge our youth are a direct result of the spiritual void in the lives of adults. Without preaching, I can tell you that my belief in the Creator and the many gifts with which the Creator has blessed me have enabled me to fulfill

my purpose here on earth. I am excited to share some of these gifts with you –
GRACE, JOY, FAITH, LOVE, HOPE, PEACE AND CHARITY, introduced in this book
as Guardian Angels. These guardian angels were created to guide you through this
developmental handbook and to watch over you throughout your lives. Each angel
has a unique personality and special purpose, just like each of you.

Adinkra symbols also appear in this book at the beginning of each chapter to
represent the relationship between where you are right now in your life and where
you will be in the future - a better place.

Adinkra is an Akan word. Akan is the language of the Akan people, who comprise
about one-half of the population of Ghana (an African country). Adinkra is the
colorful, hand-painted cloth used in Ghana by people in mourning. The Adinkra
symbols are printed on the cloths to represent the uplifting, motivating, and
character-building attributes of a deceased individual and a transition to a better
place.

INTRODUCING THE GOT IT GOIN' ON®
GUARDIAN ANGELS

Welcome to our World: A world full of Grace, Joy, Faith, Love, Hope, Peace and Charity!

GRACE (Latina) – 16 years old (Angel Color: Orange): Grace is kind, compassionate,
and forgiving. She has friends whose families are concerned about the immigration
issue, so she has agreed to do research to keep them informed and to create an
advocacy group of her peers.

JOY (Asian/Pacific Islander) - 14 years old (Angel Color: Turquoise Blue): Joy
represents supreme well-being and good spirits. She is proud to teach her friends
about her culture and traditions. She created "HUMANITY TRANSCENDS RACE &
CULTURE," a social media campaign to promote awareness and tolerance.

FAITH (Multi-Racial) - 12 years old (Angel Color: Yellow): Faith is happy, believes in her future, and trusts that she will make it through anything that comes her way. She is deaf and teaches her friends and family sign language so they can communicate with her.

LOVE (African Descent) – 17 years old (Angel Color: Pink): Love is mild mannered and confident. She is comfortable in her own skin, patient, and kind. She is a childhood leukemia cancer survivor | YAY! Her gratitude for life has created an interest in her ancestors. She is building a family tree at the Smithsonian National Museum of African American History & Culture through The Robert Frederick Smith Explore Your Family History Center.

HOPE (African Descent) – 15 years old (Angel Color: Royal Blue): Hope is street smart. She is questioning her sexual identity, and she wants to get fit. Yet, she accepts and loves who she is and has committed to becoming healthier and at peace. She believes all things are possible and is looking forward to a better tomorrow.

PEACE (Native American /Alaska Native) – 12 years old (Angel Color: Purple): Peace looks within for any answers she needs and believes in truth, honor, justice, harmony, and love. She has witnessed abuse in her family, including her sister's dating violence. She found peace while writing in her journal, which she turned into a blog to help other girls dealing with dating violence.

CHARITY (European Descent) – 13 years old (Angel Color: Olive Green): Charity is kindly and has a charitable interest in others. She is aware of and acknowledges different elements of race and power and is committed to learning about this history of ALL Americans and doing her part as an ally to make a positive change in the world.

All girls have the power to improve their lives, to overcome challenges, and not only survive but succeed and thrive with confidence. You need the right tools to help you discover yourself and what's right for you. By setting high standards for yourself and incorporating the *Standards of Excellence* introduced in this book, your opportunities to succeed in life will only multiply.

So, thumb through the book, read it slowly and do some writing, or just check out the quotes and messages throughout each chapter. There is no right or wrong way to read this book; just enjoy the journey.

A Positive Self Image will help you learn to love and respect yourself. This is your foundation for life!

Mental, Emotional, and Spiritual Fitness help you deal with life's challenges and keep your mind, heart, and spirit in one piece. *Physical Fitness* is all about being comfortable in your own skin, no matter your shape, size, or color. *Media Literacy* will explain how to be more critical about what you see and listen to, so you can make better decisions about how you navigate the media. Don't know where you're headed? *Intellectual Fitness* includes information about setting educational, financial, and career goals. You may also learn something about transitioning from middle school to high school as well as going from high school to college or career – two major rites of passage for adolescent females. Want to get along better with others? Read *Healthy Relationships/Healthy Communication.*

Do people keep asking you, *"Didn't your mama teach you any manners?"* Or are you mad that there are so many injustices going on in your community and around the world? Well, you will find social skills for Generation Z and the Alpha Generation, respectful ways to navigate the social media landscape, and learn about philanthropy, advocacy, and social justice in the chapter entitled *A Positive Place in Society.*

Young people are being destroyed and destroying themselves and each other with violence, bullying/cyberbullying, drugs, alcohol, and sex. They are acting out negatively because they have not learned positive ways of coping. When youth can't, or have not been encouraged to cry tears, they cry bullets or exhibit other self-destructive behavior. Check out *Staying Out of Harm's Way* for tips on how to say "YES!" to life and learn why early sexual activity, drugs, violence, alcohol, and tobacco are bad news.

So, you think you're cute? Well, I hope so! I certainly do! In *Looking YOUR Best*, you will find information about grooming, hair and skin care, and fashion tips that will keep you from being arrested by the FASHION POLICE! And last, but not least, *WORDS of WISDOM* is a message from girls and adults.

I am a relatively happy, healthy two-time survivor of fallopian tube cancer, the rarest of gynecologic (women's) cancers blessed with over 30 years in long-term recovery. I give to you what is within me, and I wish you all peace and success. Hopefully, this handbook will help you make positive, life-enhancing choices!

To the adults who get their hands on this book – We can make a difference if we try!

"Every day is a gift, that's why they call it the present."

Your Earth Angel Birthday

January: The Angel of Joy

February: The Angel of Understanding

March: The Angel of New Beginnings

April: The Angel of Courage

May: The Angel of Serenity

June: The Angel of Harmony

July: The Angel of Desire

August: The Angel of Reality

September: The Angel of Victory

October: The Angel of Compassion

November: The Angel of Exploration

December: The Angel of Responsibility

CONVERSATIONS WITH FAITH, GRACE, LOVE, JOY, PEACE, HOPE, & CHARITY

I AM ENOUGH!

"I AM PRECIOUS! I AM POWERFUL! I BELIEVE IN ME!"

Standard of Excellence #1

....

A Positive Self-Image
Self-love/Self-esteem/Self-respect

(Symbol of greatness)

Opening Exercise

Take a good look in the mirror. What do you see? This
affirmation is one that I have on my bathroom mirror. It helps
me start my day off right.
I hope you will use it too.

Mirror, mirror on the wall

Who's the greatest of them all?

My, oh my, it must be me –

Because I'm the only one I see!

–Have an awesome day!–

A Positive Self-Image

A person's self-image is the mental picture they have of themselves. It includes an assessment of qualities and personal worth. A simple definition of a person's self-image is their answer to this question, "What do you think about yourself?" A positive self-image is made up of several key ingredients: cultural and gender pride, self-awareness, self-love, self-esteem, and self-respect.

Positive self-image is believing in yourself and being proud of who you are, no matter your shape, size, color, hair texture, heritage, or the shape/size of your facial features.

Self-love is the most important tool in your toolbox of life. India Arie expressed it very well in her song, "Video." Here are some of the lyrics:

Sometimes I shave my legs and sometimes I don't
Sometimes I comb my hair and sometimes I won't
Depend on how the wind blows I might even paint my toes
It really just depends on whatever feels good in my soul
I'm not the average girl from your video
And I ain't built like a supermodel
But I learned to love myself unconditionally
Because I am a queen
I'm not the average girl from your video
My worth is not determined by the price of my clothes
No matter what I'm wearing I will always be India. Arie

Others of you might have heard your parents playing George Benson and Whitney Houston's song, GREATEST LOVE OF ALL – "Learning to love yourself – it is the greatest love of all."

Healthy love of self, the main ingredient in both songs, can help raise your level of self-acceptance on your journey to achieving your life goals.

Thinking more positively about yourself can help make your life more happy, healthy, and whole, no matter what's going on. During adolescence, girls, as well as boys, are searching for their identity. Adolescents need to develop a sense of self before they can master the world.

Now is the time to begin the most important love affair of your life - the LOVE AFFAIR WITH YOURSELF! Haven't you ever heard the phrase, *"If you don't love and respect yourself, why should anyone else?"*

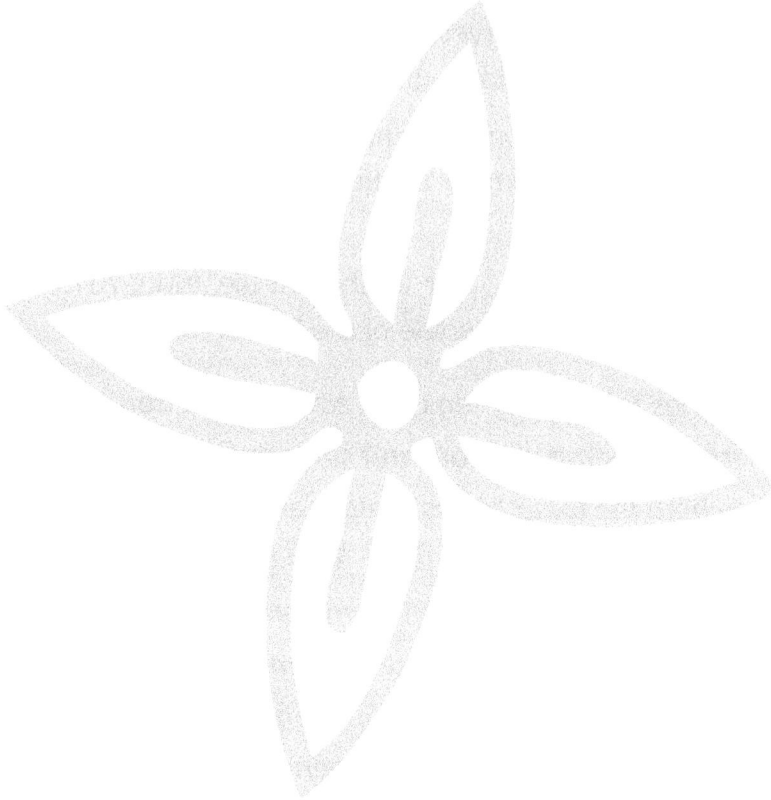

Racial, Ethnic & Cultural Pride:
What are they, and what do they mean to you?

Racial pride is being proud of your race (that does not mean you should like everything people from your race have done).

Race – A large group of people distinguished from others because of common physical characteristics, such as skin color and hair type.

FYI – the differences between human races are not great, even though they may appear to be, i.e., black vs white skin. All races of mankind in the world can interbreed because they have so much in common; that's how multi-racial children are created. All races share 99.99+% of the same genetic materials. It makes you wonder why there is so much hatred and disapproval of people who do not look like you, just because of what's on the outside. Hmmmmmm . . .

Ethnic pride is being proud of your ethnic background.

Ethnicity – Although related to race, it refers to people who identify themselves based on common ancestral, cultural, national, and/or social experiences, such as: a tribe, religious faith, or shared languages. Example: American Indian, English, Irish.

Cultural pride is being proud of the beliefs and traditions that you are raised with (unless you find them to be hurtful).

Culture – Refers to the beliefs, values, norms, and practices that are learned and shared generation by generation. Example: American, African, Asian, Indian, etc.

Learn to love yourself and where you come from, no matter what other people may think. Embrace your heritage, be it race, ethnicity, color, culture, or religion. You are who you are - find the good points and be proud of them.

We all come from different backgrounds that we need to learn about and be proud of. Investigate and learn about your own race (you might be multi-racial; learn about ALL your ancestors); ethnicity; and culture (especially if it is not part of your upbringing or school curriculum). Learn about others as well. Be aware of and accepting of other races, ethnicities, and cultures because they have all made exemplary contributions to the world.

Do not allow anyone's ignorance or fear make you feel bad about your heritage. They can do little to make you feel bad if you are already proud of who you are and where you come from. The more you know about your own history, the prouder you will be of yourself and your people. Learn the unvarnished truth about history, including the history of racism in the U.S. and the worldwide caste system.

Self-Love:
What Is It & What Does It Mean To You?
Very simply, it is the act of loving yourself.

Before you talk about yourself, let's see what a group of girls from my former Fitness & Fashion W/Funk program in Philadelphia had to say, back in the late 1990s, that still rings true today:

Self-love is:

- Acceptance and being okay with yourself.

- Being at peace with yourself.

- Wanting the best for yourself and believing you deserve it.

- Being comfortable in your own skin . . . no matter what shape, size, or color (hey, that's what I said. I guess they were listening).

Answer the questions below:

What is your definition of self-love? ....

....

....

Do you love yourself? ....

Why or why not? ....

....

....

What do you like most about yourself? ....

....

....

What do you like least about yourself? ....

....

....

Loving Others:

Who do you love and why? ....

....

....

How do you show them that you love them? ....

....

....

How do you treat them? ....

....

....

When asked this same question – "How do you treat them," the Philadelphia girls responded:

1) Do nice things for them.

2) Be there for them.

3) Buy them nice things.

4) Say nice things to them.

5) Tell them the truth.

6) Accept them just the way they are.

7) Want the best for them.

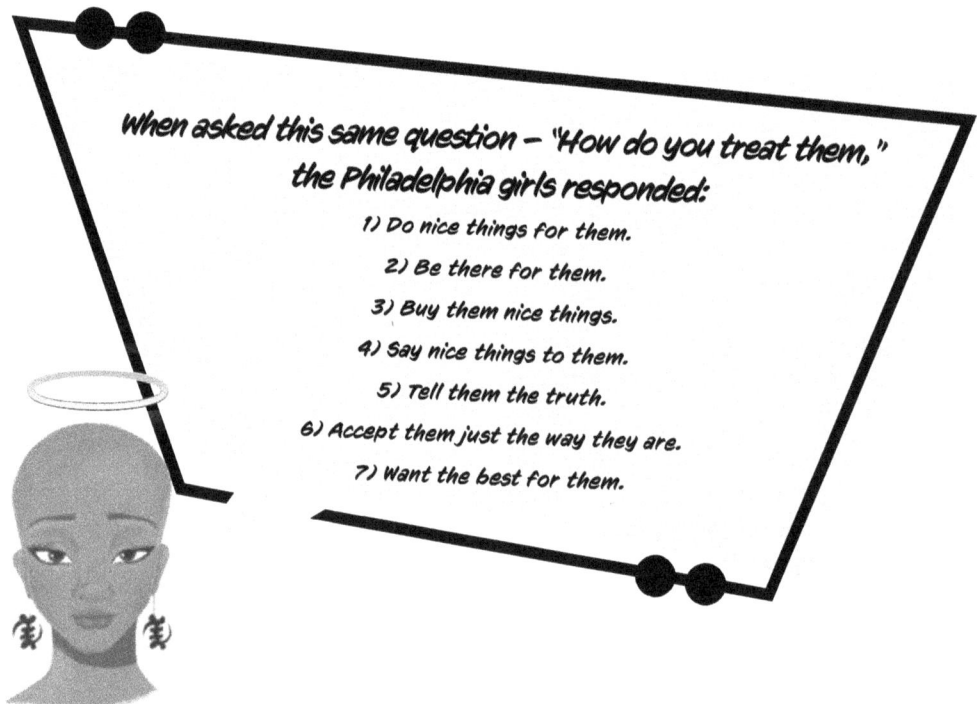

Do you do these things for yourself?

Think about your answer. If you said no, then you may need to work in this section a little longer. If you treat your loved ones better than you treat yourself, you probably have a problem with loving yourself.

Sometimes things happen which make you think something is wrong with you. It becomes hard to continue loving yourself. Here are some examples.

1. People in your life always say unkind things to you, like, *"You're ugly, worthless, or stupid."*

2. Someone has abused you or is still abusing you mentally, physically, sexually, verbally, or on the Internet, and you think it is your fault.

3. One or both of your parents are not in your life, and you blame yourself.

4. No one pays attention to you at home, in your community, or at school.

A negative self-image can lead to low self-esteem and lack of self-respect. Developing self-love, a positive self-image, and gender and cultural pride at an early age frees you from having to search for it in people, places, and things. You may know girls (or this might be you) who have a negative self-image and engage in some of the following activities:

- Drug, alcohol, or tobacco use

- Abusive or violent behavior

- Sexual activity

- Unhealthy relationships

- Posting inappropriate images on social media

- Lying and stealing

- Disrespectful behavior towards their parents and other adults

- Low self-expectations

- Low academic achievement

- Wearing inappropriate clothing

- Cursing or using other foul language

- Intimidating others (bullying/cyberbullying or stalking/cyberstalking)

- Self-isolation

No matter what a person says, you can tell a lot more about them by the way they act. When you love yourself, you make good decisions for your life. Since this book is about developing standards of excellence, we are going to discuss two other very important components for building your SELF-LOVE foundation: ***self-esteem and self-respect.***

Self-Esteem:

What Is It & What Does It Mean To You?

Self-esteem is a collection of your thoughts about you based on your life experiences and relationships. It can be high, making you feel valuable. It can be low, resulting in feelings of worthlessness. Self-esteem is determined by a combination of your positive and negative experiences and relationships in the following areas:

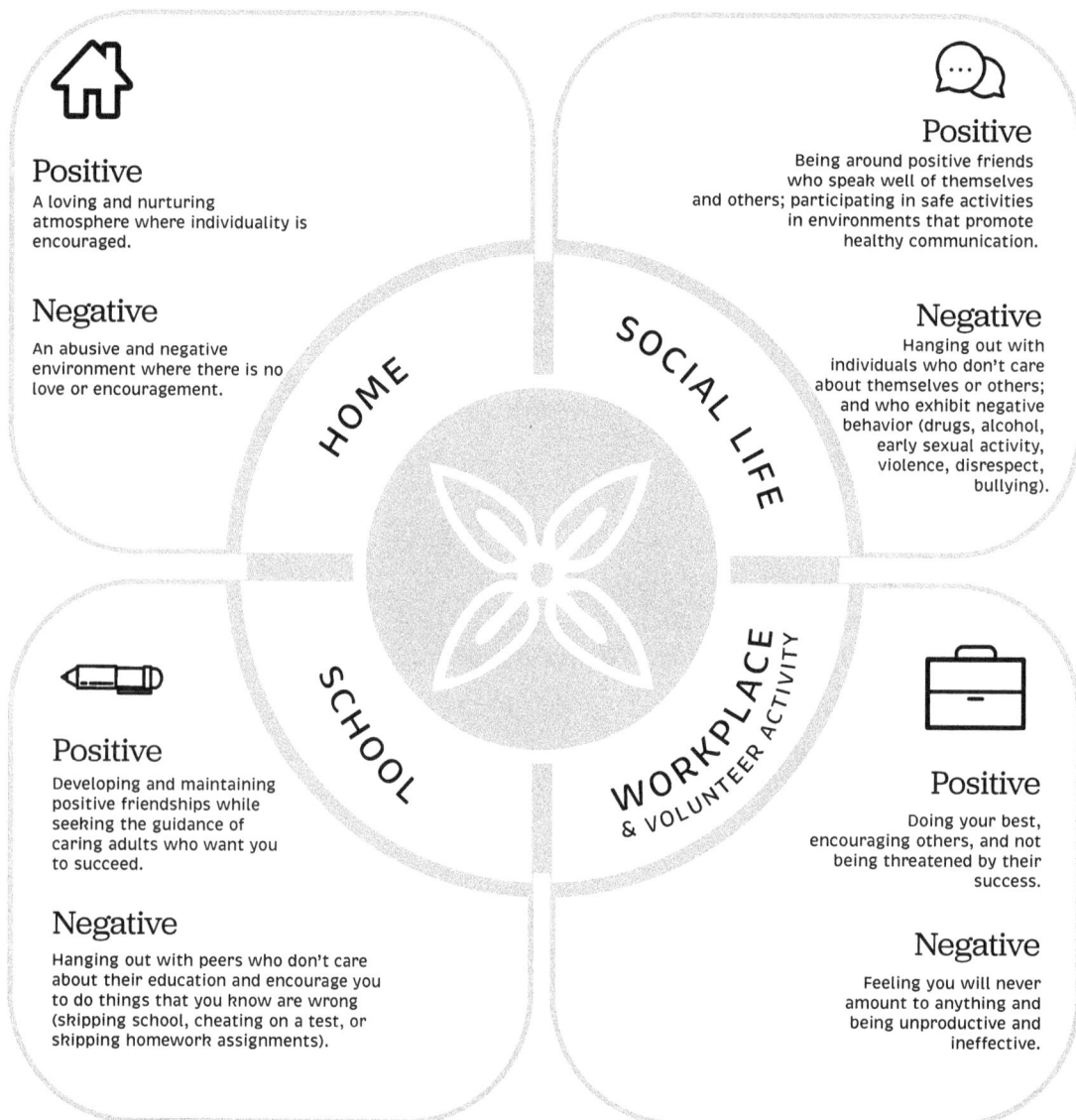

HOME

Positive
A loving and nurturing atmosphere where individuality is encouraged.

Negative
An abusive and negative environment where there is no love or encouragement.

SOCIAL LIFE

Positive
Being around positive friends who speak well of themselves and others; participating in safe activities in environments that promote healthy communication.

Negative
Hanging out with individuals who don't care about themselves or others; and who exhibit negative behavior (drugs, alcohol, early sexual activity, violence, disrespect, bullying).

SCHOOL

Positive
Developing and maintaining positive friendships while seeking the guidance of caring adults who want you to succeed.

Negative
Hanging out with peers who don't care about their education and encourage you to do things that you know are wrong (skipping school, cheating on a test, or skipping homework assignments).

WORKPLACE & VOLUNTEER ACTIVITY

Positive
Doing your best, encouraging others, and not being threatened by their success.

Negative
Feeling you will never amount to anything and being unproductive and ineffective.

In general, the more positive your experiences and relationships, the higher your level of self-esteem. On the other hand, negative experiences and dysfunctional relationships tend to result in lower self-esteem.

Even people with high self-esteem, at times, experience periods when they don't feel good about themselves. That's alright. Though it is difficult to develop higher self-esteem, the rewards are worth the effort. Let's look at some ways of improving your self-esteem.

Be Your Own Best Friend

- Accept yourself for the wonderful person you are.
- Encourage yourself. Praise yourself. Respect yourself.
- Trust your instincts.
- Love yourself. Say, "I Love You," to yourself once a day.
- Take pride in your accomplishments.
- Commit yourself to EXCELLENCE!
- Set realistic short and long-term goals.
- Always be positive. Avoid negative self-talk.
- Take pride in your individuality.
- Stop watching violent and sexually explicit movies, shows, or online performances. You become what you see and hear.
- Praise yourself, rather than waiting for others to do it for you.
- Spend a lot of time discovering more about your character/personality. Cultivate self- awareness.
- Laugh at yourself.
- Seek out SOLITUDE.
- Believe in a Spiritual Higher Power.
- Make a list of your positive qualities and keep them with you. If you are having trouble with this one, request help from someone who loves you. Realize that you are fundamentally worthy.
- Learn the "Got It Goin' On® Empowerment Pledge" and get an adult to order an "I AM ENOUGH!" Empowerment Wall Art Poster for you.
- Accept compliments.
- Make a "Thank You" or "Gratitude" list, listing people, things, and situations for which you are grateful.
- Dream, wish, hope, and pray.
- Develop plans and visualize success.
- GO FOR IT!

My Thoughts About Myself

Use this space to describe the way you feel about yourself. Be very honest. Return to this page every month and update your feelings. Take the "Got It Goin' On® Empowerment Pledge" later in this chapter. Also, get an "I AM ENOUGH!" Empowerment Wall Art Poster, so you can keep positivity all around you.

Self-Respect:

What Is It & What Does It Mean To You?

Self-respect: Loving and caring about yourself emotionally, physically, and spiritually.

You demonstrate self-respect by taking care of yourself, treating yourself with love, and by the way you allow others to treat you. Others will treat you based upon the way you treat yourself. You set the standards. ACTIONS SPEAK LOUDER THAN WORDS!

The way in which you present yourself has a lot to do with the way you feel about yourself. A positive self-image is the road to success.

A girl who has respect for herself:

- Takes pride in her body and believes it is a precious gift. She does not mistreat it or allow others to mistreat it (drugs, alcohol, violence). She does not engage in early sexual activity and learns to understand the beauty and responsibility of this adult activity.

- Takes time to get to know and accept herself.

- Develops good hygiene and grooming habits.

- Carries herself with dignity and grace.

- Has gender and cultural pride.

- Does not chase after others or disrespect others' relationships with their partner.

- Develops good health and fitness habits.

List five other things that show self-respect:

1.

2.

3.

4.

5.

List five things you do that show that you respect yourself:

1.

2.

3.

4.

5.

How can you tell when a girl does NOT have self-respect?

1.

2.

3.

4.

5.

Do you exhibit any of the signs of a girl who has low/no self-respect? If so, please spend more time on this section and then move on. It can help if you re-read this section weekly for several months. It can also help if you talk with a positive role model about how you can improve your self-respect using the tips from the beginning of this section – **"A girl who has respect for herself."** If your self-respect is solid, just keep these tips in mind as you continue through the handbook and your life.

How can you increase your self-respect?

I am glad you asked that question:

1. Develop a strong sense of self. Spend time with yourself and figure out what is important to you. What do you stand for - what is your bottom line? Learn about your heritage. Heritage is a person's unique, inherited sense of family identity: the values, traditions, culture, and artifacts handed down by previous generations. We absorb a sense of our heritage throughout our lives as we observe and experience the things that make our family unique. Knowing your heritage is a great way to find yourself.

2. Learn to love yourself just the way you are.

3. Engage in positive, age-appropriate activities.

4. Surround yourself with positive people who speak well of themselves, you, and others. Build and maintain relationships with happy, healthy, and whole adults who genuinely care about young people/adolescent females.

5. Remove yourself from negative people and situations.

6. Stop blaming others! Take responsibility for every aspect of your life.

I Am Enough!

Girls are one of the world's most precious natural treasures.

NO! Is a complete sentence.

Become SELF-AWARE.

I am beautiful, healthy, special, loveable, peaceful, powerful, strong, and safe. I MATTER!

Dance, sing, bathe, floss, and travel.

I love, accept, adore, and cherish myself unconditionally, for the awesome girl I am - RIGHT NOW!

(Excerpts from the GIGO/I AM ENOUGH! Empowerment Art Poster)

Got It Goin' On® Empowerment Pledge

I Am Enough!

I pledge to honor my body, mind, and spirit, and to make life-enhancing decisions that give me opportunities to achieve my goals. I will use the skills I learn from the Got It Goin' On-II personal development handbook to improve my overall well-being. To honor my body and increase my opportunities, I will participate in activities that increase my knowledge of sexual health, substance abuse, dating violence, and social media exploitation.

Your Signature: ....

Parent/Guardian Signature: ....

Date: ....

"Speak LIFE to ALL girls . . . for they become what you tell them!"

www.janiceferebee.com

Respect For Others

Respect for Others: Because of a love and belief in yourself, you can treat others with kindness.

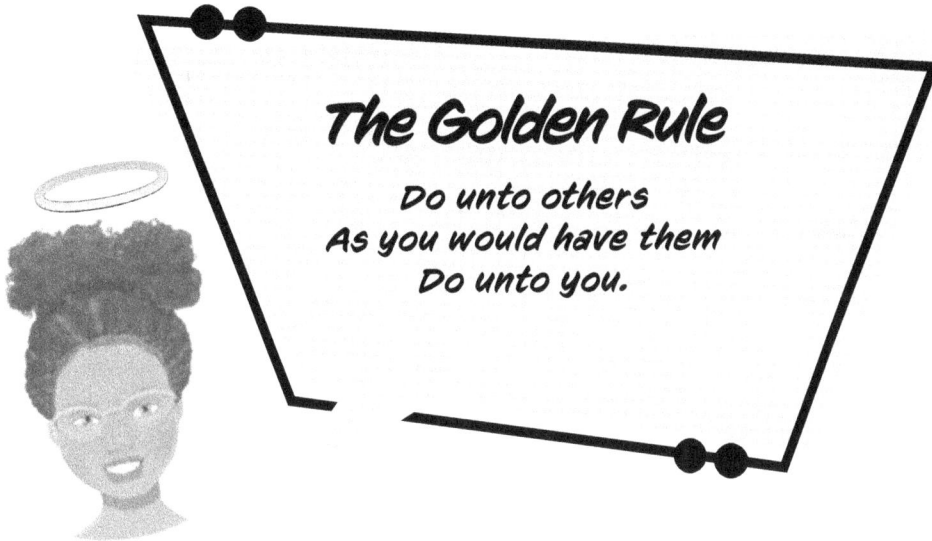

The Golden Rule

*Do unto others
As you would have them
Do unto you.*

Regardless of whether you like a person, it is always important to treat them with respect.

You show respect for others when you:

- Listen to someone else's opinion, even when you don't agree.
- Allow a much older, younger, or disabled person to have your seat on public transportation.
- Use good manners (please, thank you, excuse me, etc.).
- Use proper online etiquette when using online platforms like Facebook, Instagram, Snapchat, TikTok, Twitter, YouTube, etc.

List some other ways you show respect for others:

1. ....

2. ....

3. ....

4. ....

5. ....

"DIS"-respect: What does it mean to be "disrespected" or to "disrespect" someone?

When you disrespect someone, you treat him or her unkindly, call them out of their name, or intentionally say something mean or rude. A person who is disrespectful usually has low self-esteem. They feel as though they must put someone else down to make themselves feel better. If someone disrespects you, respond respectfully without lowering your standards. If you feel threatened or need additional support, find an adult.

List some disrespectful behaviors:

1. Cussing (cursing) someone out.

2. Putting negative or inappropriate comments and/or images on social media platforms.

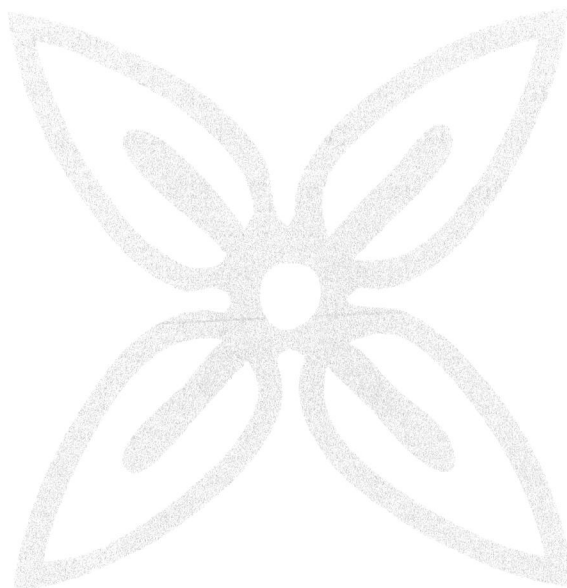

3. ....

4. ....

5. ....

Values:
What Are They & How Do They Affect Your Life?

Values: The beliefs people choose to live by (the things that are important to you). Everyone has their own set of values, which are influenced by their own environment.

What is important to you? What do you value?
Rank ten values that are important to you.
(Add to the list and rank in order of importance to you.)

1. Making your own decisions ....

2. Time alone ....

3. Honesty ....

4. Education ....

5. ....

6. ....

7. ....

8. ....

9. ....

10. ....

The following people, places, and things can influence a person's values. How do they influence YOUR values?

Explain:

1. Classmates (peers):

2. Parents/guardians, caregivers, & family members:

3. Society (media/social media, community, and religious leaders, etc.):

4. School counselors, teachers, coaches, and other school staff:

How do your values affect your actions concerning the following?

1. Tobacco, alcohol, and other drugs:

2. Violence and other anti-social behavior:

3. Relationships with individuals and sexual activity:

4. Relationship with family and friends:

5. Social media/navigating the Internet & other digital technology platforms:

6. Your future:

Decision-Making

Decision-making: Making up your mind about an issue based on information you have gathered, your personal experiences, your values, and sometimes what other people say.

Steps to making a good decision:

1. Identify the problem, situation, or issue.

2. Gather the facts.

3. Evaluate your options. Be honest and thorough.

4. Look at both the negative and positive consequences.

5. Make a choice that you can live with.

6. Take action/do something!

Learn to deal with your decision and to evaluate the outcome. This will help you in the future when the situation presents itself again. You may need to do something differently, or you may choose to do the same thing again because it worked for you.

List three situations where you had to make an important decision. What did you do and what was the outcome?

1. ....

2. ....

3. ....

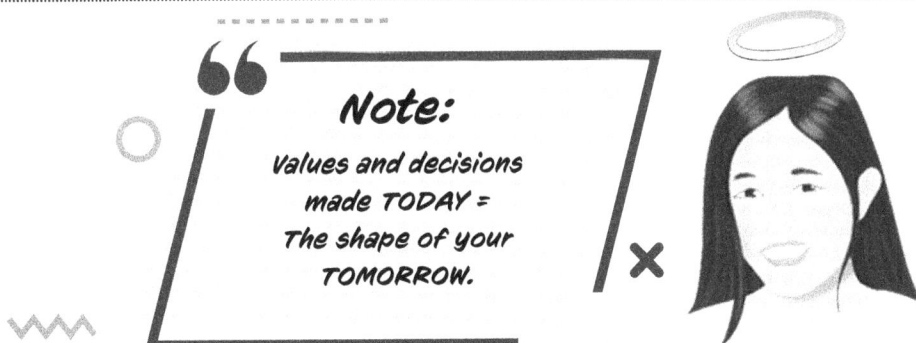

Note:
Values and decisions made TODAY = The shape of your TOMORROW.

A Page For Your Positive Thoughts

(END OF CHAPTER CHECK-IN!)

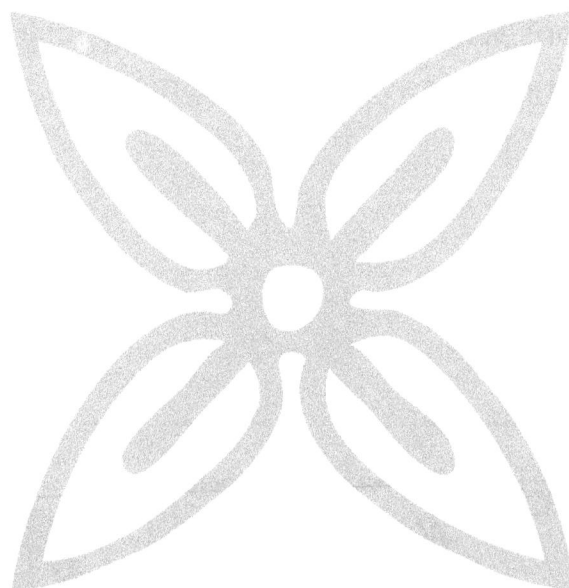

Closing Affirmation:
Be Kind To Yourself And To Others!

CONVERSATIONS WITH FAITH, LOVE, PEACE, AND HOPE

I have learned to be happy just the way I am, even though I can't hear. I know some people think it's a handicap, but you have to learn to deal with the life you're dealt...I did!

Wow! It is really challenging dealing with all of the things going on in the world today.

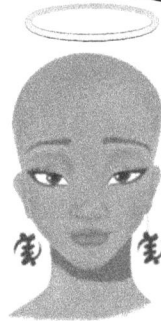

I know--
School is really different now. Girls are talking about me on social media, and I feel sad all the time.

I know what you mean. I have witnessed some crazy stuff at home and thought I would go crazy. I got help and now have some tools to cope with my life. You can too.

"My inner spirit gives me peace.

I can handle any problem I face."

✠ ✠ ✠ ✠ ✠ ✠ ✠ ✠ ✠ ✠

Standard of Excellence #2

....

Mental, Emotional, And Spiritual Fitness
Dealing with Life's Challenges

(Symbol of spiritual balance and strength)

Opening Exercise

Listen to your favorite soothing song with your eyes closed. Think about how wonderful the world is and how wonderful you are already. List ten wonderful things about you.

1. ....

2. ....

3. ....

4. ....

5. ....

6. ....

7. ....

8. ....

9. ....

10. ....

Mental, Emotional, And Spiritual Fitness

Mental fitness: healthy in your mind.
Emotional fitness: healthy in your heart.
Spiritual fitness: healthy in your soul.

Mental, emotional, and spiritual health, like a positive self-image, are invisible tools evidenced by the way you are living. Young people need to develop healthy minds and learn good habits to keep their minds fit. Learning healthy ways to cope with everyday life, as well as not-so-everyday life, can help make your life more meaningful.

Mental Fitness:
What Is It and How Does It Affect Your Life?

Mental Fitness: Healthy in your mind. Healthy thoughts and coping skills for different situations.

Adolescence can be a wonderful period. It is the time between puberty and young adulthood (ages 10-19). It can also be turbulent, but most adolescents get through with few scars.

During adolescence, you will deal with many new experiences, such as relationships, decisions about your future, and physical changes in your body. The way you deal with these experiences will depend on the way you feel about yourself and the way you cope with these changes.

Girls who learn healthy ways of handling life's challenges are better equipped to handle situations when they get older. Girls who seem to have trouble coping with life will have a difficult time, and may need some extra support. Seek out a compassionate adult who is willing to listen to your problems and concerns. School group counseling sessions or programs with other girls who are dealing with the same issues may also be a good option for you.

Now, let's discuss some of the most difficult issues facing girls of color in the 21st century and healthy ways you can prepare to deal with them.

Difficult Issues Facing Teen Girls

Abuse (mental, physical & sexual)	*Depression*
Grieving	*Discrimination*
Alcohol or Other Drugs	*Eating Disorders*
Incarcerated Parent/Caregiver	*Peer Pressure*
Catastrophic Natural Distasters or Other Tragic Situations	*Racism*
Parent/Caregiver in the Military	*Sex Trafficking*
Peer Aggression (Bullying & Cyberbullying)	*Stress*
Suicide & Cyberbullicide (suicide directly or indirectly influenced by experiences with online aggression).	*Covid-19*

Unfortunately, girls of color face increasing challenges which threaten to derail their futures. There are many resources available to help you. Let's see what you can do right now.

Tips for Coping with Life's Challenges

Improve your self-image, self-esteem, confidence, and cultural pride. It will help you face the challenges of adolescence, peer pressure, hate, racism, and changing responsibilities.

1. Dealing with Depression

Depression is a disturbance in your mood where you may feel particularly unhappy, discouraged, lonely, or negative towards yourself. It is important to understand that depression happens to all of us at different times.

You can become depressed about the way you look, peers making fun of you, loss of a loved one, moving and leaving your friends, getting bad grades, family break-ups, a parent/caregiver going to jail, a parent/caregiver in the military and away from home, a break-up with a significant other, racism, or, upon hearing about, watching, or experiencing a catastrophic or tragic situation (like the murder of George Floyd by a police officer and the COVID-19 global pandemic, which both occurred in 2020). Depression is a natural experience, but you must cope with it in healthy ways, so you don't stay depressed. If you cannot shake those bad feelings, you may need professional help. Depression is a treatable illness.

For those of you on Facebook and other social media platforms, new research has found a possible link between Facebook and depression, so be mindful about the time you spend online and your emotions. They say, *"with in-your-face friends' tallies, status updates and photos of happy-looking people having great times, social media pages can make some youth feel even worse if they think they don't measure up"* (American Academy of Pediatrics, 2011). We'll talk about this more in the Social Media section of this book.

Symptoms of depression:
- Changes in behavior
- Loss of appetite or over-eating
- Sleeplessness or sleeping too much
- Loss of interest in school and/or your regular activities

Coping strategies for depression:
- Develop a good support system of friends and family – people you can talk to.
- Talk to them when you feel good and when you feel bad. Get professional help if necessary.

- Learn to minimize stress. Here are some things you can try: Exercise and eat regularly, get enough sleep and have a good sleep routine, have regular *me* time and *friend* time, and take some deep breaths.

- Accept yourself for the wonderful person you already are!

- Get out and help someone.

- Understand that life is full of the expected and the unexpected, both of which you must learn to accept. Let someone know you are in pain.

If you feel that your friends might make fun of you, seek the support of a caring adult, or a professional, or call **The National Suicide Prevention Lifeline Number (1-800-273-8255)** to speak to a trained counselor without having to give your name (anonymously) if you are feeling hopeless and overwhelmed.

2. Dealing with Grief

Grief is the natural reaction to a personal loss or major life change. For recovery purposes, the stages of grief include:

- DENIAL,
- ANGER,
- BARGAINING,
- DEPRESSION, and
- ACCEPTANCE

For some teens, experiencing grief can be difficult. Sometimes, adults close to you or your peers don't understand your sadness. Breaking up with a parter after dating them for a short time, or the death of a pet, may not seem significant to others but can be to you. It is important to have time and space to experience all the stages of grief. This will enable you to have closure and to move forward.

When the grieving process is interrupted, some teens find unhealthy ways of coping – starving (anorexia), vomiting (bulimia nervosa), overeating, drinking, taking drugs, engaging in inappropriate sexual activity, and when it gets bad – getting stuck in the depression stage, which can turn to suicide.

Coping Strategies for Grief:

- Learn about the stages of grief and talk with a caring adult about them. Get professional help if necessary.

- Allow yourself time and space to go through each stage of the grieving process.

- Develop self-value and self-worth early in life, so that life's disappointments and tragedies do not devastate you.

- Develop a belief in a power greater than yourself and a belief that you can survive life's challenges.

- Find joy in your life and recall happy memories about the people, places, or things that you lost.

3. Dealing with Negative Peer Pressure

Negative peer pressure is the subtle or obvious pressure from friends to do things you don't feel good about. Although peer pressure can be powerful, it is not as powerful as positive parental or other adult influence.

*Peer aggression (bullying) includes physical, verbal, relational, and cyber aggression. It is important that both youth and adults understand that all forms of adolescent peer aggression MUST be taken seriously, both at school and at home, and that online harassment can have grave, real-world consequences.

- **Physical:** Harm through damage or threat of damage to another's physical well-being.
- **Verbal:** Obvious and/or hidden verbal aggression toward another, such as threats, put downs, and name-calling.
- **Relational:** Behavior that is intended to harm someone by damaging or manipulating his or her relationships with others.
- **Cyber:** Online bullying – like writing nasty comments about someone on the various social media sites like Facebook, Instagram, SnapChat, TikTok, Twitter, etc.

Coping Strategies for Negative Peer Pressure:

- Respect yourself and your values.
- In the face of negative peer pressure, stand up for yourself.
- Believe in yourself and do your best to develop what's called "grit" – a combination of passion and striving toward an important goal (like doing well in school or self-respect).
- Become friendly with positive adults.
- Choose positive peers – young people who think well of themselves and have positive plans for their future.

Why Do Girls Bully?

Although this kind of destructive behavior can begin as early as preschool, it tends to get more attention in adolescence. Girls can bully in packs or alone. Those who choose groups tend to form cliques with girls for safety, popularity, and sometimes because they have things in common. FYI – All cliques are not negative. Girl bullies often are themselves rejected by peers and lack meaningful relationships. These girls learn how to manipulate others, especially if they don't feel good about themselves.

Some characteristics of a girl bully are jealousy, feelings of superiority, poor impulse control, low self-esteem, and lack of empathy. Girls generally bully when they don't get their basic needs met:

- Acceptance (by self)
- Belonging (among others)
- Control
- Meaningful existence

Some girls will do what they need to do to get these needs met, even if that means hurting you.

What to Do If You See Someone Being Bullied

It might not be happening to you, but you may have the unfortunate experience of seeing others being bullied. You might think it's okay to just stand and watch or to ignore the bullying. But try to think – what if that was you? Here are several suggestions from *www.girlshealth.gov* of things you can do to make a difference:

- Stand up for the victim: It takes a lot of courage, but it could help. Be careful not to put yourself in danger.

- Don't join the bullying: If the bully tries to get you to join in refuse, walk away, or surprise the bully and defend the victim.

- Stop the rumors: Don't help spread rumors. You wouldn't want others to spread rumors about you. Don't listen. Let the rumor stop with you.

- Tell an adult: Don't just stand there and watch! Tell/go get an adult, especially if someone is being hurt physically. If you feel unsafe, ask the adult to keep your comment private.

What to Do if You Are Being Bullied

You feel good about yourself most of the time and don't try to make others angry, at least not on purpose. But it happens anyway – you are being bullied! What should you do? Here are a few suggestions from *www.girlshealth.gov* that might help:

- Tell an adult: Some girls don't want to tell because they think they might be seen as a snitch. Adults can help stop the bullying only if they know about it.

- Stand up for yourself: Practice being confident. Even try out what you would say to the bully with a friend or adult.

- Do not fight back: "Easier said than done!" But, if you give in, you might be the one to get in trouble. Do your best to walk away or ignore the bully. If you are being hurt physically, try to yell for help and get away fast, and get help from an adult. Defend yourself if all else fails.

- Make new friends and get involved: This will help you feel better about yourself. Make sure you choose positive friends who are free of bullying.

- Be strong: Bullies like to pick on people who can't stand up for themselves. Having good self-esteem and confidence goes a long way. Sometimes you may have to *"fake it until you make it"* and the next time a bully picks on you, you will be confident for real!

What If YOU Are the Bully?

Many girls are bullies in school and outside of school. Ask yourself if you have ever repeatedly hurt someone because they were younger, weaker, different, or less confident than you. If you determine that you are a bully, here are some suggestions from *www.girlshealh.gov* of things you can do to stop:

- Recognize and admit that you are a bully and that your actions are hurting people.

- Talk to a trusting adult: Talk to an adult or school counselor to learn how to get rid of your bullying behavior. They will be proud of you for wanting to change.

- Form healthy relationships: Learn about what healthy relationships look like.

- Choose positive people your age, as well as adults.

- Put yourself in their shoes: How do you think you would feel if you were being bullied? Try to understand how it makes them feel.

- Make a change: Change your behavior and be kinder to yourself and others.

Take the quiz at www.girlshealth.gov to find out if you are a bully.

4. Dealing with Stress

Stress is pressure from within yourself, or from outside sources, that causes you to be anxious.

Common causes of stress:

- Changes in your life at school or at home
- Social situations
- School pressures
- Parental expectations

Signs of stress:

- Lack of concentration
- Bad attitude
- Continuous sickness
- Not eating or eating a lot
- Constant anger
- Cutting

Coping strategies for stress:

(These are also good for girls who are not under stress, but want to develop good stress management skills.)

- Learn relaxation techniques.
- Participate in things you enjoy.
- Try closing your eyes and breathing deeply while listening to soothing music.
- Exercise and eat healthy foods.
- Ask for professional help if you need more support.
- Talk with positive peers and/or adults.
- Stay away from drugs, alcohol, or other mood-altering chemicals.
- Learn to recognize when you are becoming angry. Develop constructive ways to control and express your anger, including taking an anger management class.
- If you are cutting: Become aware of the stressors that trigger your cutting.
- Make plans to do something healthier when you get the urge to cut; perhaps something that will soothe or calm you.
- Start a journal listing all the things that bother you. Write in your journal on

a regular basis, and it will become a healthy habit.

- Work to discover ways to express the deep anger or pain you may be feeling (Journaling, music, poetry, walk, or a self-defense class).

- You can get help for self-injuring behavior. If these suggestions don't help, seek professional help through a trusted adult. YOU ARE WORTH IT!

5. Dealing with Youth Suicide, Cyberbullicide, and Prevention

Youth suicide is when a young person deliberately ends his or her own life.

Cyberbullicide is suicide directly or indirectly influenced by experiences with online aggression (Hinduja & Patchin, 2009). This section is not meant to scare you, but it is very important to understand suicide and the benefits of a healthy mental and emotional attitude. Perhaps you can prevent someone from wanting to go there – that someone could be YOU!

Factors That Increase the Risk of a Suicide Attempt:

- Being bullied or being a bully

- Alcohol or drug addiction

- Previous suicide attempt

- Social rejection

- Peer pressure

- Peer aggression

- Depression

- Family history of abuse, suicide, or violence

- Loss of limb, blindness, deafness, or terminal illness

- Unrequited love (when someone you love doesn't love you back)

- Fear of ridicule for getting help for a problem

- Exposure to other teens committing suicide, such as at school or in the media

- A belief that suicide is noble

- A recent loss such as a death, break-up, or parents' divorce, illness, or disability

- Access to firearms or other lethal weapons

Possible Suicidal Warnings:

- Depression

- Substance abuse

- Frequent episodes of running away or being in jail

- Family loss or instability; significant problems with parents

- Discussions of suicidal thoughts, or death, or the afterlife during moments of sadness or boredom

- Withdrawal from friends and family

- Difficulties in dealing with sexual orientation

- Lack of interest in previously enjoyable activities

- Unplanned pregnancy

- Impulsive, aggressive behavior or frequent expressions of rage

Some girls who think about killing themselves usually feel alone, hopeless, and rejected. They are more likely to feel this way if they have been bullied, experienced a loss or trauma, performed poorly on a test, broke up with a significant other, are having concerns about their sexual identity, have abusive or addicted parents, or have experienced parental separation, divorce, or death. However, you could still be suicidal even if none of these conditions existed.

A Few Important Suicide Statistics

- Suicide is the third leading cause of death among young people ages 15-19.

- Each day, 14 young people (ages 15-24) commit suicide or approximately 1 every 100 minutes.

- Experiencing racism is associated with thoughts about suicide for Black youth and adults.

- Depression, sadness, and suicide of Black girls and young women is on the rise – suicide rates among Black girls ages 13-19 nearly doubled from 2001 to 2017.

- Among adolescents, LGBT youth attempt suicide 3 times the rate of heterosexual youths. Source: December 31, 2014 – Special Reports, Psychiatry, Gender Issues.

- Cyberbullying victims were almost twice as likely to have attempted suicide compared to youth who had not experienced cyberbullying.

What can you do to help yourself through these crazy, mostly fun years of adolescence so that ending your life is not an option?

Coping Strategies for Preventing Suicide

- Build your self-esteem. Believe in yourself and your value to this world.

- Surround yourself with people who think you are wonderful.

- Develop healthy coping strategies for stress.

- Learn to trust positive peers and caring adults.

- Develop healthy outlets for anger.

- Find joy in your life, even if your surroundings are full of drama.

- Look deep within yourself to find purpose for your life.

- Find something you are passionate about.

- When your goals or dreams don't work out, create new ones.

    (Source: KidsHealth.org – The Nemours Foundation)

What can you do if you are feeling suicidal or know someone who exhibits some of these traits? List some ideas.

1. Immediately talk to someone you trust or call a hotline!

    (THE NATIONAL SUICIDE PREVENTION HOTLINE: 1-800-273-8255).

2. ....

3. ....

4. ....

5. ....

I cannot stress enough the seriousness of this topic. We all have value and a purpose to fulfill. If you are gone, we will never know how awesome your contributions would have been.

Are you or any of your friends experiencing these or other challenges?
If so, how are you dealing with them?

....

What are some of your coping strategies?

....

Have you ever used a hotline? _____ Yes _____ No

If yes, for what, and did you get the help you needed?

....

Do you have positive peers and/or caring adults in your life?

....

I hope this section has given you some things to think about. Now that we have talked about being healthy in your head let's talk about being healthy in your heart and soul. But first, here's a message from a friend:

"I want to leave you with some ways for you to deal with as well as overcome your problems in life – Prayer. After praying, try talking to someone – a teacher, family members, peer mediator, or a friend. Make sure that what you are talking about is kept between you and that person. Try using my technique of writing down your feelings and then writing a poem. Expressing your feelings may be hard, but if you believe in a Creator and don't give up, it will come easy. May the Creator continue to be with you and bless you and your family. Remember, anything or anyone can change with a power greater than yourself. I would also like you to keep in mind what has been passed on to me, "I cannot, I will not, I shall not, give up!"

--LaDonna Russell

(Former Teen Ministry Member Metropolitan Baptist Church, Washington, DC)

SPIRITUAL FITNESS:
WHAT IS IT and HOW DOES IT AFFECT YOUR LIFE?

Spiritual fitness is also important. Spirituality is the essence of who you are, your inner being, and your belief in the Creator. In other words, your spirit is that small voice inside you that is always with you and always knows the truth; the truth about who you are and who you are not (self-awareness). Your spirit knows your purpose and wants the best for you. She is your guide to greatness, and she wants you to find her and believe in her.

Spiritual Fitness: Taking good care of your soul. It is about the importance of nurturing and pampering yourself so that you can live a comfortable, joyous, and peaceful life. Having a relationship with your Creator.

Many girls are taught to take care of others. They grow into women who are overworked, unhappy, and unhealthy. Now is the time to learn about self-care or pampering. I am not talking about grooming. I am talking about spending time, alone, to help you get in touch with who you are and developing a relationship with your Creator. Slow down, chill out, and think – WITHOUT DRAMA!

There is a difference between grooming and pampering. Grooming is external, mostly physical and tends to focus on improving outer appearance. You may look good but not feel good. Pampering is an inside job. Pampering focuses on the inner self, treating yourself with extreme care and attention. Pampering makes your soul smile.

Here are some things you can do to pamper yourself:

- Talk to the Creator - ask for strength and guidance.
- Take a bubble bath with soft, soothing music.
- Get away from everyone and enjoy quiet reading time.
- Make a list of things that bring you joy.
- Take a quiet walk in a safe place and think.

You may think that you are too young to do any of this stuff, or to even understand it, but you are mistaken, my young friend. The sooner you learn that you are a special being with a special purpose, and become aware of your inner qualities, the sooner you will understand the importance of taking good care of yourself.

Self-awareness is the ability and willingness to recognize both your strengths (good points) and weaknesses (not so good points). Accepting the good, the bad, and the ugly about yourself helps you to admit that you are human, just like the rest of us. Making a commitment to build upon your strengths and work on correcting your weaknesses enables you to become all you can be and to take care of your inner self.

Let's find out about your strengths and weaknesses:
List some of your strengths
(the things you are good at or positive character traits):

1. I am friendly.

2. ....

3. ....

4. ....

5. ....

List some of your weaknesses (areas that you feel need improvement):

1. I easily get an attitude.

2. ....

3. ....

4. ....

5. ....

When you know who you are, no one can take advantage of you. So, take time and fill in all the blanks and add more if you would like. Come back to this exercise if you are unable to complete it right now.

Affirmations can be very helpful.

An affirmation is a positive statement that has the power to change who you are and your possibilities. Affirmations are powerful because they allow you to create a new person, different from the person you are right now. Four qualities of effective affirmations:

1. They are stated in the present tense - no past or future tense.

2. They are personal. Use "I" and refer to change in yourself, rather than in someone else.

3. They are stated in the positive - don't use the words not, won't, or don't.

4. They are to be repeated - say them frequently over a long period of time. Changing old thinking can take time.

Here are examples of affirmations. After reading them, create a few of your own. After you have listed them, put them in places where you can see them, like your bedroom or bathroom mirror or inside your notebook or journal.

EXAMPLES

- I deserve to take good care of myself.

- My body is a divine creation deserving of tender, loving care and attention.

Now you try:

MY AFFIRMATIONS - Replace negative thoughts with positive ones.

- I am a special girl with unique gifts.

- I am a beautiful girl.

- ....

- ....

- ....

What Brings Me Joy?

Do you ever sit quietly and watch the trees blow or listen to the birds sing, watch "Too Cute," or a funny movie on your favorite streaming platform, or inspiring Tik Tok videos? Here are some things that bring me joy.

Add to the list.

- Dancing and singing to music all by myself.

- Praying (talking to my Higher Power) and meditating (listening for my Higher Power's response).

- Spending quiet time with myself.

- Writing in my journal.

- A good meal with family and/or friends.

- Hugging a child!

- ....

- ....

- ....

- ....

- ....

Closing Exercise

Take time, right now, to sit still and just be with yourself.

Think about how special you are. If you don't feel special, say positive affirmations several times a day. It may take a little longer for some, but one of the most rewarding results of self-care is that it rubs off on others.

When you take good care of yourself, even at a young age, you are more relaxed and able to cope with life. People want to be around you and will probably ask for your secret.

You are Special & Kindness is Free! Spread it Everywhere!

A PAGE FOR YOUR POSITIVE THOUGHTS

(END OF CHAPTER CHECK-IN!)

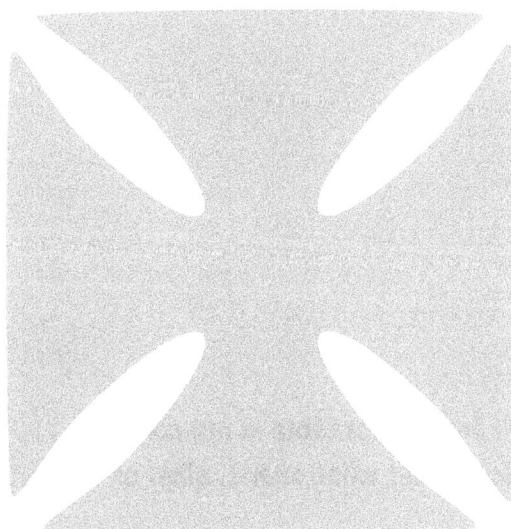

CONVERSATIONS WITH HOPE AND JOY

Girl Chef! Can't wait to start eating better, learning about the cooking business, and teaching other girls. Need to start excersising too. LETS DANCE!

I'll be your first customer! Try making food from different cultures. I heard that food brings people together. Also, let's start a DANCE group so we can all get fit.

"I am comfortable in my own skin . . .
No matter what shape, size, or color."

‡ ‡ ‡ ‡ ‡ ‡ ‡ ‡ ‡ ‡

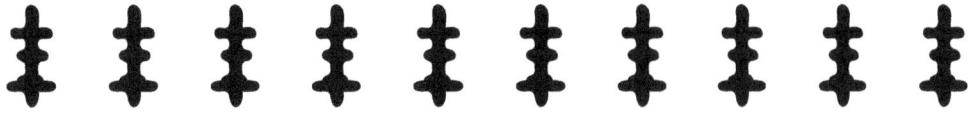

Standard of Excellence #3

....

Physical Fitness & Nutrition

Being Comfortable in Your Own Skin
Work That Body!

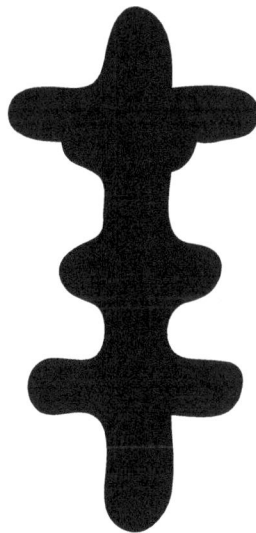

(Symbol of strength, bravery, and power)

I am especially excited about this ***Standard of Excellence***, given that I have worked on maintaining my own physical health ever since I was your age! My passion for fitness and desire to share that passion with girls led me to start a program in Philadelphia called *Fitness & Fashion with Funk*. That program transformed into the award-winning *Got It Goin' On® Empowerment Program for Girls*, which was featured on *The Oprah Winfrey Show* in 2001 and won an *ESSENCE* Award. Now that I am over 60 – FIT, FIERCE, AND FABULOUS – and have experienced the benefits of good physical health (even after conquering cancer, twice, and alcohol and drug abuse) and witnessed girls in the program feeling and looking better, I encourage you all to make time for fitness and good overall health!

Take time during this chapter to determine what you like and make it part of your life-long plans to stay fit. Concentrate on the importance of exercise and healthy eating. Both should become a permanent part of your daily habits. Add good mental health and you have the ingredients for a healthy lifestyle that works FOR YOU!

PHYSICAL FITNESS:

What Is It And How Does It Affect Your Life?

Physical Fitness: Being in the best shape for YOUR BODY. This includes regular exercise and proper nutrition that will enhance your overall health. This combination can help you live a long and relatively disease-free life.

Many girls are worried about their bodies - are they too fat or too skinny or something else. First, it is important to take a good look at yourself. Your body will go through many changes over the next few years. As you grow, get to know your body, make friends with it, and be thankful for it. Unless you have a lot of money for plastic surgery, I encourage you to accept the wonderful body that your Creator gave you.

Your body is a precious gift, no matter what shape, size, or color. How you treat it and what you do to keep it healthy has a lot to do with the image you have of your body. Let's talk more about Body Image. Everyone has an inner view of their outer selves. This mental picture is known as body image. Healthy body image and self-esteem go hand in hand. And, despite what many people think, Black girls and other girls of color do have body image issues just like White girls. As adolescent females, your bodies are growing and changing. Perhaps you're self-conscious and overly aware of every pound and pimple. That's normal. Body image can be positive or negative and is influenced by different things. How do we learn about body image? There are many ways. Here are two of the most popular ways:

Family: If you receive positive comments about your body, you will have a healthier attitude in life. Negative comments can make you feel inadequate. Too much emphasis on appearance gives you the idea that your looks determine who you are.

The media: TV, movies, magazines, songs, videos, advertisements, the internet, and social media – are constantly sending messages that say what matters most is how you look. They promote either unhealthy body images, usually thin (only 4% of the world is naturally built like a super model), unrealistic shapely standards (booty and boobs), or unhealthy portrayals of female sexuality and unnecessary nudity that can become overwhelming. This is powerful stuff. Girls begin to see their bodies as sex objects, or objects of beauty, instead of nature's finely tuned machine. This misperception can lead to eating disorders, low self-esteem, depression, and unrealistic and sometimes dangerous desires to achieve media perfection, sometimes through the desire for plastic surgery. But you can fight back – you are powerful! The good news is that you can learn to positively navigate through these crazy years and develop a positive body image no matter what your shape, size, or color. Most importantly, learn to value yourself more for who you are than what you look like.

How is your BODY IMAGE? Answer these questions honestly.

1. Are you self-conscious about the way you look?

   ....

2. Do certain parts of your body bother you a lot? If so, which ones?

   ....

3. Do you frequently compare yourself to other girls or women on social media, actresses on television, in movies, or in magazines?

   ....

4. Do you repeatedly check yourself in mirrors or avoid them all together?

   ....

If you answered "yes" to any of these questions, you may need to work on your body image. Setting goals is important, but you must first learn to love yourself just the way you are.

When the Obsession for a Media Perfect Body Takes Over– It Can Lead to the Desire for Plastic Surgery:

A) Some girls find fault with their bodies and the way they look and make the decision to alter their physical appearance by going under the knife and having plastic surgery. Be careful that you are not getting caught up in this appearance driven culture, the enormous popularity of reality TV shows, or your teenage hormones that tend to make some girls obsessed and dissatisfied with their bodies. These are natural feelings as you grow up - even I got teased for being flat-chested. I'm comfortable with my small breasts today, and there is no race for them to hit my waist as I age.☺

B) Although, for many years, plastic surgery for some teen girls meant a nose job (still the most popular), doctors are reporting an increase in chemical peels, otoplasty (ear surgery), breast, butt, and chin implants, liposuction, and tummy tucks to girls as young as 14. Be very clear - plastic surgery is NOT a quick fix for popularity or self-esteem. Don't believe the hype - cosmetic surgery is NOT the magic answer to changing your looks and your life. This is serious stuff!!! Do your best to learn to love the YOU that was put on this earth.

When the Obsession for a Media Perfect Body Takes Over - It Can Lead to Eating Disorders:

A) Some girls find it hard to accept the natural changes their bodies are going through, like the necessary added fat due to hormones and puberty. Some are faced with negative peer pressure and academic pressures. Others receive negative body image messages from dysfunctional family members. And others are heavily influenced by the overload of thin young celebrities and become destructively fearful of weight gain. Although it was thought that only White girls suffered from this issue, Black and Latina girls suffer as well. This can lead to mistakenly feeling forced to get rid of the unwanted weight any way they can. These feelings can lead to eating disorders, which are experienced by 1 or 2 out of every 100 youth.

B) What is an eating disorder anyway - and when does a diet become a disorder? Eating disorders are extreme eating behaviors - the diet that never ends and gradually gets more restrictive, for example. Or when a person can't go out with friends because she thinks it's more important to go running to work off a snack eaten earlier.

C) You have probably heard of anorexia and bulimia. They are the most common eating disorders. The full names of the disorders are Anorexia Nervosa and Bulimia Nervosa. Girls with anorexia and bulimia often have an intense fear of becoming overweight or think they are overweight even when they are not. But there are other food-related disorders, like binge eating and body image dysfunction that can lead to serious problems - even death. The good news is that they can be treated if caught early enough.

If you or someone you know is suffering from an eating disorder, find a trusted friend or adult to share with so you can get the help you need. It is especially important for girls of color to be aware of this type of body image issue because it is not very widely talked about in minority communities. Black and Latina girls are thought to all love the curves they might be developing. That is a myth. There are still a good number of girls of color who are influenced by mainstream standards of beauty and turn to purging (throwing up) in order to be thin.

Body Image Revisited:

Now that you have some information about how family, along with media images and messages, can influence and affect how you feel about your body and how far some girls take it, let's revisit the opening exercise – HOW IS YOUR BODY IMAGE?

1. Are you still self-conscious about the way you look?

    ....

2. Do certain parts of your body still bother you? If so, which ones?

    ....

3. Do you still frequently compare yourself to other girls, including girls on social media, actresses on television, in movies, or in magazines?

    ....

4. Do you still repeatedly check yourself in mirrors or avoid them all together?

    ....

5. What have you done/are you doing to help you become more accepting and loving of your body?

    ....

It's going to take time, so be patient and gentle with yourself, and learn to love yourself just the way you are.

Here are some tips to develop a healthy body image, and put your energy towards more important things:

1. Know how you feel about your body.

2. Develop a greater appreciation of the human body by finding beauty in all shapes and sizes.

3. Wear clothes that are comfortable and pleasing. This increases your physical comfort and can help bring you some peace and acceptance.

4. Find positive adult role models and talk to them about their body image and how they developed their attitudes.

5. Find out about their eating and exercise habits and how they may have overcome their own negative body image -- if they struggled with that.

6. Develop skills that have nothing to do with appearance. Focus on your achievements, accomplishments, and things you do well.

(Some of the information in this section came from the Body Image brochure created by the Office of Health Education and Promotion, Health Services at the University of New Hampshire.)

Resources to help support the information in this section:

www.kidshealth.org/teen/ (Body Image)

http://teens.webmd.com/girls-puberty-10/girls-eating-disorders

https://www.theguardian.com/commentisfree/cifamerica/2009/apr/07/african-american-women-bulimia

More Than a Body: Your Body is An Instrument, Not an Ornament | Dr. Lexi Kite and Dr. Lindsay Kite

The Body Image Book for Girls: Love Yourself and Grow Up Fearless | Charlotte Markey

Healthy Girls Rock!

Now that you know what healthy is, it's time to learn some tips to get and keep your body healthy.

Your Weight

What's Healthy for Your Height?

Depends on:
- Height
- Age
- Body type and composition
- Rate of growth

Other factors may come into play but let's start with these.

Don't compare yourself to another girl who is the same height and age because different things are going on in her body from yours. Here's a great resource to do your own research *www.kidshealth.org/teen/food_fitness/*.

The best place to learn about your ideal healthy weight is your doctor. Since they know your family history and your specific growth information, they are the best source.

What About Obesity?

As a result of eating too much unhealthy food and not moving enough, the world has become a place filled with children, youth, and adults who are overweight, many of them dangerously so - better known as obesity. Obesity is defined as excess body fat. If you are an obese girl, know that you are a gift and worthy of love just like every other girl. Because you are so precious, it is important to find out what is causing your overeating leading to your obesity. It could be caused by family shopping, eating and exercise habits (don't be one of those girls who won't exercise because they don't want to mess up their hair), lack of healthy food in your community and/or school, and/or emotional issues. There are also girls who are obese due to no fault of their own. Their hormones are not balanced properly, or medication necessary for an illness may cause weight gain. Do your best to get help to get to the bottom of your weight situation so that you can get on the road to healthy habits. Your life is worth living - in a healthy body!

HEALTH

H_2O

Are You Getting Enough Sleep?

Did you know that teens should get 8 to 9 hours (or more) sleep to be prepared for a productive day at school? Research has found that teens are on a different body time clock than children and adults, and many times teens are so busy they don't get the required amount of sleep. First, be mindful that you are not SUPERGIRL and although you may have many essential responsibilities, start learning now how to manage your time responsibly. Lack of sleep, in teens can result in the following:

- Inability to pay attention in class
- Falling asleep in class
- Poor grades
- Inability to do your best in athletics

- Drowsy driving leading to accidents/death
- Emotional troubles such as sadness and depression

Here are some suggestions to getting a better night's sleep:

- Set a regular bedtime
- Create the right sleeping environment (quiet, dark)
- Exercise regularly
- Avoid stimulants after 4:00 p.m. (caffeine, energy drinks, and tobacco - please stop smoking NOW!)
- Relax your mind
- Don't nap too much during the day
- Avoid all-nighters

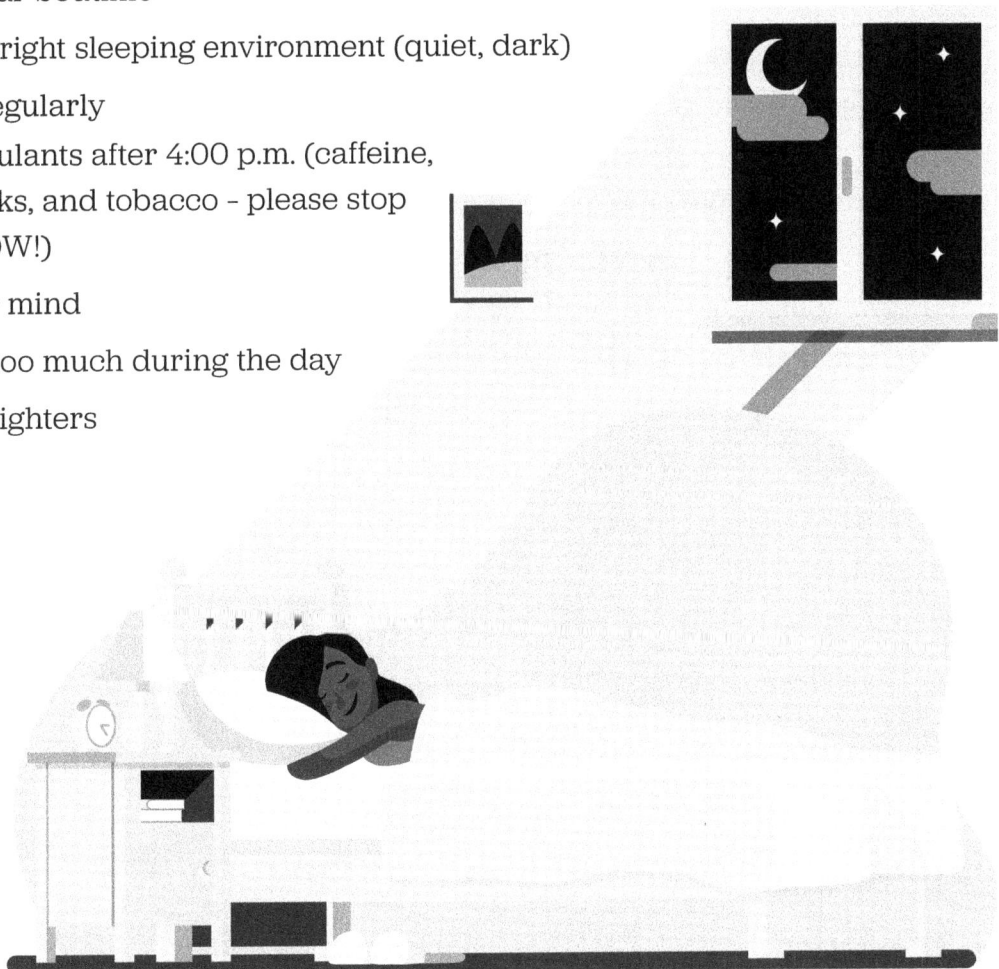

EXERCISE/PHYSICAL ACTIVITY

Did you know there is a relationship between physical activity and positive self-esteem? "Athletes involved in sports tend to have higher levels of self-esteem, happiness, confidence, and academic achievement since sports regularly offer a sense of accomplishment. Sports -- anything from tennis to Double Dutch to stepping - is an ideal way to enhance overall health and fitness." (Women's Sports Foundation)

Here is more information from The President's Council on Physical Fitness and Sports Report: Physical Activity & Sport in the Lives of GIRLS:

- More girls are participating in a wider array of physical activities and sports than ever before.

- Exercise and sport participation can enhance mental health by offering adolescent girls positive feelings about body image, self-esteem, success, and self-confidence.

- Research suggests that physical activity can help reduce the symptoms of stress and depression among girls.

Okay, you have no excuse. This research was just for you! But don't take my word for it, get out there and do your own research. Remember that every exercise program should include aerobic activities to strengthen your heart and lungs and muscle and bone strengthening exercises as well. Examples of this type of exercise are listed below. Circle the ones in which you participate and add some of your own.

PHYSICAL FITNESS ACTIVITIES

1. Swimming	14. Lifting Weights
2. Basketball	15. Inline Skating
3. Volleyball	16. Soccer
4. Walking	17.
5. Track	18.
6. Tennis	19.
7. Stepping	20.
8. Jumping Rope/Double Dutch	21.
9. Gymnastics	22.
10. Golf	23.
11. Dancing	24.
12. Rowing	25.
13. Fencing	26.

So, you see, there are a lot of activities. It is important to choose something you like and incorporate it into your daily lifestyle. Making time for physical activity should become a priority in your life. Find ways that are going to help you get moving.

Are there obstacles in your life or in your community that keep you from becoming active? Is your school's physical education program weak or nonexistent? Is your neighborhood too dangerous? Were you affected by COVID-19 and couldn't go outdoors very much? Or are you just lazy? This can be a problem. If you or someone you know wants to be more active, there are a few things you can try:

- Exercise along with regularly programmed television or online programs, go to TikTok, or find a good app. *DON'T LET ANY EXCUSES KEEP YOU FROM EXERCISING!*

- Dance like crazy in your room for 30-60 minutes every day to your favorite music!

- Walk around the neighborhood with a friend if it is safe.

- Start a Double Dutch, stepping, or dance club.

- Get involved in or start a *Got It Goin' On®* *"GIRLS*TALK!"* program in your community.

Do your best, regardless of your situation. It may be difficult, but don't give up. Create your own exercise routine and make it a priority and the beginning of a lifestyle for your future. Physical fitness experts suggest daily exercise for 60 minutes each day for girls ages 12-17. Fill some of your idle time with physical activity or make special time in the morning or evening for aerobic exercise (getting your heart rate up) or strength training (resistance/weights). Go ahead – I dare you to be creative!

Resources (choose your own if these are no longer available or you want to try something else):

Teen Diaries: "Pretty Girl Rock" Dance Workout - https://www.youtube.com/watch?v=h4wFxplj8o8

30-Minute Hip-Hop Tabata to Torch Calories: https://www.youtube.com/watch?v=kwkXyHjgoDM

Easy Exercises for Teens: https://kidshealth.org/en/teens/easy-exercises.html

Meet the 80+-Year-Old Bodybuilder -- Ernestine Shepherd (Born June 16, 1936): https://www.youtube.com/watch?v=hpBo2dl3PBc

NUTRITION FOR ADOLESCENT GIRLS

Did you know that your body, to grow and be healthy, needs food?

Now we're going to talk about nutrition and developing good eating habits. You should strive for good eating habits and a regular exercise routine. It's never too late to start. As with each **Standard of Excellence,** try to find adult role models who are happy, healthy, and whole.

They can help you establish your own healthy lifestyle.

Being physically fit, in addition to exercising, means putting the proper fuel into nature's finely tuned machine -- your body. I have seen young people eat so much junk food it makes me want to scream. For your body to develop to its full potential, and to help prevent disease, it is important to eat healthy foods in amounts that are healthy for YOUR body.

Did you ask me what was healthy? Before I answer that, let me give you some nutrition facts. Did you know? . . .

- Freshly squeezed orange juice (fresh or frozen) is particularly good for teenage girls.

- Teenagers typically eat five to ten times more sodium (salt) than they need.

- The rate of teen obesity has more than tripled since 1980.

- Whole milk, cheese, hamburger meat, bologna, and ice cream are five of the worst foods for teens due to high saturated fat content.

(Source: CSPI - Things for and About Kids)

Some of you already have healthy diets while others are literally killing themselves by not eating properly. If you just opened the book to this page, know that you are a precious gift and deserve to live a long and healthy life. The information on these pages is meant to help you live a life that is happy, healthy, and whole.

Did you know that bariatric surgery/band and gastric bypass (weight loss surgeries) are on the rise in teens? Our youth are going to die young if they don't take hold of their weight!

Look at the new Food Plate, which has replaced the Food Pyramid in the US to help Americans remember how to eat a balanced and healthier diet. If you don't already, see if you can start balancing your diet according to the new Food Plate. Depending on your age, you may need some guidance. Remember, this food plate only suggests ways to balance your diet.

Keep a journal of your eating habits for one week. List the food that you eat all day long for one week – healthy and not so healthy. Don't cheat – this exercise will help you see your habits and support you in making better food choices in the future. Come back to this section of the book after the week and see how your diet compares to the Food Plate. Going forward, try to make better food choices based on the Food Plate.

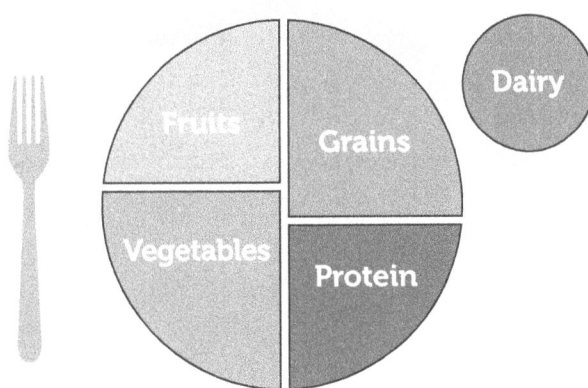

Healthy Foods

1. Fruit
2. ....
3. ....
4. ....
5. ....
6. ....

Not So Healthy Foods

7. Chips
8. ....
9. ....
10. ....
11. ....
12. ....

You have the power to change your eating habits. Close your eyes and visualize that wonderful body that was created to take you through a lifetime. Are you really taking care of it when you throw in greasy, salty, or sugar-filled junk food? Your body is a precious temple. Think about all the time you spend, especially as you get older, making the outside look good -- clothes, hair, maybe make-up. Don't mess it up by putting all that garbage into it.

Here is some information that should help with choosing the kinds of food you eat.

Ten of the Worst Foods for Young People

- *Soda*
- *Hamburgers*
- *Hot Dogs*
- *Ice Cream*
- *Bologna*
- *Whole Milk*
- *American Cheese*
- *French Fries and Tater Tots*
- *Pizza loaded with cheese & meat*
- *Chocolate Bars*

Ten of the Best Foods for Young People

- *Fresh fruits & vegetables (especially carrot sticks, canteloupe, oranges, watermelon, and strawberries)*
- *Cheerios, Wheaties, or other whole-grain, low sugar cereals*
- *Extra-lean ground beef*
- *Whole wheat crackers*
- *Chicken breasts and drumsticks without skin or breading (not fried)*
- *Skim or one percent milk, almond milk, coconut milk, goat milk, or rice milk.*
- *Seasoned air-popped popcorn*

(Source: CSPI - Kids Stuff)

Yes, I know the second list doesn't sound very exciting. I'm not saying you must give up all sweets or foods that may be high in fat or salt content. Just don't eat them every day, all day. EVERYTHING IN MODERATION!

Remember, you are still developing. While you are still young, it is very important to establish good exercise and eating habits - make it a lifestyle, so it becomes part of your life at an early age. Please start now!

FYI: There is really no mystery to the sudden mood swings that surprise many teenagers and shock the adults around them. It is as simple as a sugary cereal eaten for breakfast or empty snacks after school, says nationally known pediatrician Dr. Lendon Smith. *"Up to 90 percent of teen-agers' mood swings, surliness, drowsiness, and general anxiety can be attributed to their diet,"* says Smith.

CHOW!

Resources:

www.kidshealth.org/teen

www.choosemyplate.gov

www.fda.gov/media/78628/download (Spot the Block: Using the Nutrition Facts Label to Make Healthy Food Choices -- A Program for Tweens)

www.fitness.gov/10tips.htm (10 Tips to Healthy Eating and Physical Activity for You)

www.hopkinsmedicine.org/health/wellness-and-prevention/healthy-eating-during-adolescence

http://www.girlshealth.gov/nutrition/healthyweight/bmi_calc.html (Body Mass Index Calculator)

http://www.girlshealth.gov/ (Girls.Health.gov)

http://www.fueluptoplay60.com/ (Fuel Up to Play 60)

http://win.niddk.nih.gov/publications/take_charge.htm (Take Charge of Your Health: A Guide for Teenagers!)

A PAGE FOR YOUR POSITIVE THOUGHTS
(END OF CHAPTER CHECK-IN!)

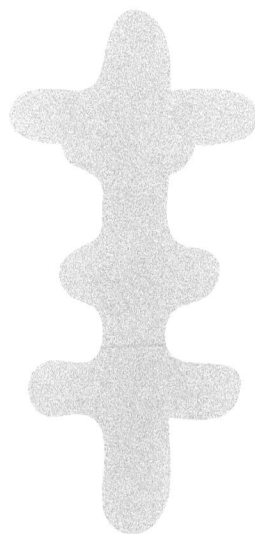

CONVERSATIONS WITH LOVE, GRACE, PEACE, CHARITY, AND JOY

You know you cant believe everything you see and hear these days? Learn where information is coming from and if it is a trusted source.

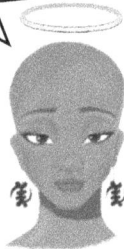

We need to make sure all media is in different languages so we can all communicate and understand.

We must find a way to counteract all of the negative media images, messages, and influences girls face every day. Seems like the world has gone mad!

Lets make sure to show self respect and respect for others when on social media. We can even help others using social media by becoming advocates for girls around the world!

We can make more responsible media choices when we learn about media literacy. We can also learn to create our own content with new digital platforms. Sounds like fun to me!

"I am critical about what i see and hear."

Standard of Excellence #4

Media Literacy

Counteracting "CRAZY!"

Negative Media Images, Messages & Influences

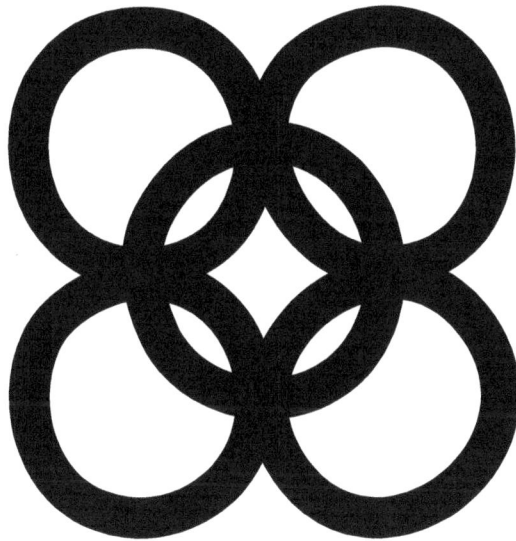

(Symbol of pride of state and at the same time a warning against an inflated pride or an inflated ego.)

MEDIA LITERACY: WHAT IS IT and HOW DOES IT AFFECT YOUR LIFE?

Media literacy is the ability to access, analyze, evaluate, and create media. Media literate girls are better able to understand the complex messages they receive from television, radio, Internet, newspapers, magazines, books, billboards, video games, music, and all other forms of media. Being media literate can also provide more equal opportunities in digital environments.

Media literacy has also been defined as a host of life skills that you need to fully participate in our media-saturated, information-rich society. In this digital age, it's important to have skills to do the following:

- Make responsible choices because of being able to locate and share the materials you find, as well as understand that information – whether you find it online, in a book or magazine, see it on television, or hear it on the radio.

- Analyze messages – find out who wrote it, understand why they wrote it and their point of view, and evaluate the quality and credibility of the content. Just because someone says something doesn't make it true or what you believe.

- Create content in different forms – being able to properly use language, images, sound, and new digital tools and technologies.

- Be mindful of how you behave and communicate when using new technology – have a sense of self-respect and respect for others.

Advocate – take social action by working individually and with others to share knowledge and solve problems in the family, at school, and by participating as a member of a community.

Having these practical skills is important for daily navigation through life. For example – 1) If you want to apply for a job online, you need to have the skills to know what to look for and where to look for it; 2) If you don't like what you see on television, what you hear on the radio, or what you read in a magazine or newspaper – be able to take action, write to the people in charge, and demand a change. The more people complain, the better chance you have to make something happen.

In addition, because of how dependent we are on digital forms of communication, it's even more important for you, as adolescent females, to develop these skills so that you can make better decisions about how you allow the media to shape your thoughts and what you can do to change things you don't like. This is called *advocacy*. It's also equally important to find a balance between engaging in media-related activities and activities that get you out and moving.

Girls are bombarded with all types of media images and messages every day and everywhere - some positive/appropriate and some negative/inappropriate. Without knowing it, you can become influenced by those images and messages. That's what is known as subliminal messaging - like how a commercial can get you to purchase products you might not even need. Positive images and messages (in commercials, songs, videos, magazines, online, etc.), will most likely influence you to engage in positive behavior and present yourself in appropriate ways. If the images and messages are negative or inappropriate, the opposite is likely - you can be influenced to engage in negative behavior and adopt inappropriate attitudes. The media has the power to influence you in a negative or positive way.

SOCIAL MEDIA & GIRLS:

Popular Social Media Platforms:

Facebook: A social media website.

Instagram (IG: IGTV & Reels): A simplified version of Facebook, with an emphasis on mobile use and visual sharing.

Pinterest: An image sharing and social media service to help you discover ideas and information.

Snapchat: A multimedia messaging app used globally.

Tik Tok: A music video social media platform.

Twitter: An online news and social networking site where people communicate in short messages called "tweets."

YouTube: An online video sharing and social media platform.

WhatsApp: A messaging app that lets users text, chat, and share media.

What's New . . . ?

Be VERY careful what you share on any of these platforms. Don't be surprised if your parents/guardians insist on monitoring your social media. It's for your own safety. You shouldn't be posting anything you wouldn't want them to see anyway.

SOCIAL MEDIA EMPOWERMENT CHALLENGE:

Here's something you can do to lift your confidence and your spirits.

Pick one month and share a positive *"I AM"* statement on your social media platform(s) for each day of the month. You can even add a positive, powerful image with the statement. Share with your friends and have a challenge to see who can complete it with new empowerment statements each day.

Example: Monday - *I AM* Healthy; Tuesday - *I AM* Intelligent; Wednesday - *I AM* Creative.

How girls are impacted

With social media and everything happening online, girls can be overwhelmed with what they see. It can have both positive and negative consequences, which is why it is critical that you learn how to evaluate this type of communication that has taken over.

Positive:

- Girls can connect with others like themselves, so they don't feel so different.
- Girls can communicate with others around the world.
- It's important to stay safe online and not share too much information.

Having access to different media outlets can help raise political and cultural awareness in girls. It can provide exposure to news as well as information about other cultures and help to dispel stereotypes. It can provide increased awareness of the world around them and open them up to innovative ways to give back.

Social media can help in the development of social skills. With positive communication, girls can widen their social networks, boost social confidence, and heighten their knowledge of media literacy.

Girls can use social media to make their voices heard about something they like or don't like.

Negative:

- Too much time spent online can cause stress and physical complaints and conditions.
- Snapshots of the popular, rich, and famous can cause unrealistic expectations and can set girls up for extreme disappointment.
- Can cause "body shaming"
- Self-Objectification

Constant status updates and picture perfect airbrushing programs can cause increased anxiety and depression.

The focus is on appearance more than achievement

- Digital Drama - like cyberbullying

- Sexting and Sexploitation: Sharing compromising images, like partially nude pictures or pictures of you doing things like twerking.

- Glorifying Negative Behavior - Television, music, movies, and online shows often show and glamorize characters using drugs, alcohol, tobacco, and engaging in inappropriate/risky sexual or violent behavior. Girls are developing and need to understand that this is not reality. It's up to parents and other responsible adults to teach you about the negative consequences of inappropriate or risky behaviors and the false images often promoted in the media to make money. That's why it's so important for you to learn to use your critical thinking skills, and responsible adults can help by talking to you about the difference between reality and fantasy.

- CAUTION: It is extremely important that you understand the dangers of sharing personal information, like where you live or go to school, or about other family members like younger siblings, and posting inappropriate pictures, like using the middle finger. It's also important for you to understand that once you post something on social media it's there forever, even if you delete it - things can come back to haunt you later - like when applying for a job or school.

It's very important to be prepared before you dive into the digital media world.

Since this is how your generation communicates, take the time you need to learn how to protect yourself and how to be critical of what you see and hear.

I'm going to end this chapter with some insights from Mirabel Tran, a former student at Marina High School, who wrote a blog article in the Huffington Post/Teen – 4.21.2014:

1. Social media is prevalent in society today, and it has been scientifically linked with causing depression in young girls.

2. Depression is linked with obesity in young girls.

3. Obesity is also linked with lower grades in young girls.

4. Ultimately, social media is affecting the health and education of young girls nationwide.

"Needless to say, I think that the best and most effective solution is to empower young girls to control the effect that social media and advertisements can have, rather than simply putting the blame on capitalistic companies who want to market their product. We need to invest in young girls around the world, and especially the United States, to use their intelligence and minds as tools and resources to achieve their goals and dreams, rather than using their bodies. To all teenage girls around the world, I want you all to know that you girls are all beautiful, no matter what age, shape, size, height, or race. You are strong, you are amazing, and you will not be defined by what society markets as "beautiful."

I want you to believe in your self-worth, and I believe that the best kind of beauty lies in the hard work and determination that you put into your dreams and goals, whether it be in making yourself look good (for yourself, of course!) on a Friday night or pouring your heart and soul into an essay.

We are all strong, but we are stronger together, and I hope that you can spread and share the message in this post to the people you love... the people that don't believe in their own unique beauty."

A PAGE FOR YOUR POSITIVE THOUGHTS
(END OF CHAPTER CHECK-IN!)

CONVERSATIONS WITH FAITH, LOVE, PEACE, HOPE, GRACE, JOY & CHARITY

I know my purpose and want to use my gifts to help other deaf youth.

I am glad I listened to my mentor a few years ago and took the time to set some goals for my life. You are never too young!

I don't like exercising but I'm trying to hang out with girls who do different stuff to stay physically active. We are creating a schedule for the rest of the school year and beyond.

I know how to hustle in the streets, but that's not for me anymore. I'm going to use the money I make from my cooking business to start saving to open my own restaurant - after culinary school, of course.

I will be the first in my family to graduate from high school in the U.S. It's been hard, but I'm planning to go to college.

I have pretty good relationships with girls of different races and cultures. I hope I will stay in touch with them as I get older.

Believe it or not, girls can grow up to be anything! We can be pilots, teachers, doctors, electricians, and even President! We already have a female vice president...what's stopping us?!

"I Am Preparing For My Future Because I Believe In My Tomorrow."

$ $ $ $ $ $ $ $ $ $ $

Standard of Excellence #5

....

Intellectual Fitness for
The Digital Generation

Setting Goals: Personal, Relationship, Educational,
Financial, Career, Physical & Spiritual

(YOUR Personal Best)

(Symbol of strength, bravery, and power)

WHAT DOES YOUR FUTURE HOLD?

Many girls don't have a clue about their lives beyond today. Some girls have no plans because they do not believe they will be alive. That's very sad. I hope you will embrace your life and look forward to a wonderful future, no matter what your situation.

In this digital era, having "grit" will take you a long way. Grit is a fancy word for learning how to be persistent and sticking with something over a long period of time until you master it. Most times, girls who have this trait can overcome challenges, deal positively with failures and difficulties, and achieve the goals they have set for themselves. There is so much for you to experience and achieve, but you must have goals and a plan of action. This chapter discusses the importance of setting goals in several areas of your life - **personal, relationship, educational, financial, career, physical, and spiritual.**

Your **personal goals** are probably THE most important. This includes establishing general short and long-term goals. Your personal goals will help you determine your career, educational, and financial direction.

Relationship goals are focused on your interactions with others. Consider what you can do to improve your relationship with people who are important to you. Also, consider what types of people you want to meet and how you can develop positive relationships with those people.

Educational goals are important as well. Whether you are an "A" student or struggling with your grades, you need to set goals as to what you want to achieve in school. Just remember, always strive for excellence - YOUR PERSONAL BEST! If you have good grades and want to maintain them, there are some tips that will help you. Developing educational endurance and grit will help you right about now. If you are struggling to get a "D," hang in there, help is on the way. Most of all, it's important to want to do your best. No one can want more for you than you want for yourself. In the age of COVID-19, distance learning has caused challenges to educational achievement that no one could have imagined. Try your best to focus and get help when needed.

Your **financial future** will depend greatly on developing a respect for money and learning to manage it. The more you know about the value of a dollar and how to save, invest, and spend wisely, the richer you will be, both in the bank and in your spirit. You can watch your savings grow by saving a portion of the money you get from your allowance (if you get allowance), odd jobs, or money gifts from birthdays or other special occasions. Spend $60, instead of $160, on sneakers, start a small business, or learn how to invest in the stock market.

Career goals are important, too, especially if you are approaching the end of high school. If you have some idea about what you want to do when you get out of school, it will be easier to plan your future. Whether it's going to be a vocational career institution (cosmetology, electrician, construction, cooking, etc.) or four-year institution, having some idea about what you want to do in life will help a great deal. Some of you already know your purpose; others are still trying to figure it out.

When you are sick or not feeling your best, you are not able to fulfill any of your goals. Your *physical health goals* are important. Strive for the best physical health possible for you. Make a choice to exercise for at least 30 minutes, 5 times each week. Make a choice to eat a well-balanced diet to include a portion of dairy, fruits, vegetables, grains and protein (see **Standard of Excellence #3**).

Have you ever asked, why was I created? What is my purpose? Your *spiritual health goals* are related to your purpose and why you were uniquely created (see **Standard of Excellence #2**). Consider your unique gifts and talents (what you naturally do well) as you consider your spiritual goals. Ask yourself – How do I want to use my gifts and talents to advance my collective goals, this includes your personal, educational, financial, career, physical, and spiritual goals?

Exercise

Find seven people who have goals, one for each category: personal, relationship, educational, financial, career, physical and/or spiritual health goals. Ask them to share two goals with you. Have them sign their names and write their goals in the space provided below. This exercise will help you see the different goals people set. You may want to use them as role models when you start setting your own goals.

NAME	GOAL
1.	
2.	
3.	
4.	
5.	
6.	
7.	

WHAT DO YOU WANT TO ACHIEVE IN LIFE?
Setting Personal Goals

You can do and be anything you want! If only more girls believed that. Do you know what you want in life? Now is a great time to start thinking about that. The exercises included in this section are to make you think about your life and encourage you to act. **That goes for younger girls, too.**

My Personal Goals

Listed below are samples of personal goals. If you can think of others, add them to the list. Update this information four times a year. I have provided a form to get you started. Use your phone or tablet to input reminders on your calendar to update/revise/review your goals. Keep your responses simple and make this exercise fun.

1. Your *relationships* - Are you getting along with your parents/caregivers, siblings, friends, authority figures, (and when you get older, a person you like) and how do you strengthen those relationships?

2. Your *finances* - Do you want money for a new digital device, clothes, school, a car, a place to live, or a trip? Do you want to be wealthy when you get older? Do you want to be financially independent? Do you want to invest in the stock market? Do you want to save or raise money for a business? Is contributing to your church important to you? Well, how are you going to afford these things? Find a good financial literacy program for young people, like *OPERATION Hope* or Angel Rich's *Get Wealthy Life* resources.

3. Your *education* - Do you want to pass your next test, pass to the next grade, get back in school, graduate from junior high or high school, go to college or trade school, or just learn something new? What steps do you take?

4. Your *career* - What do you want to be when you grow up? Do you want to own your own business, or run someone else's? Think about what you enjoy.

• Making jewelry to sell to your friends, baking or cooking, doing hair/nails, writing poetry, or coding could be the beginning of a business empire!

5. Your *physical health* - Do you want to live a long, healthy life? Do you have any bad habits you need to stop? Do you exercise regularly and eat healthy foods? Do you like the way you are developing and want to maintain your good health habits? Do you want to lose weight or just get in shape? You can do it!

6. Your *spiritual health* - Is your life full of chaos and confusion? Do you want inner peace? Do you want to know yourself better? Do you want to develop a relationship with your Creator? Do you have a bad attitude and want to change it? Praying can help. Yoga and meditation, as well – you can learn.

My Goals

	3 Months	6 Months	1 Year	5 Years
My Relationships				
My Money				
My Education				
My Career				
My Physical Health				
My Spiritual Health				

Take time to do this exercise – it's a great lesson in time management and responsibility. I recommend inputting this into your digital devices to keep track of your goals. Work with your friends or an adult. Suggest that your entire class participate. You are now on the road to planning your future.

Resources:

OPERATION Hope: www.operationhope.org

The Wealth Factory, Inc.: www.getwealthylife.com

Ways to Build Student Stamina: www.soniclearning.com.au/how-to-build-student-stamina/

ARE YOU MAKING THE GRADE?
Educational Goals

Now, let's spend a little time on your educational goals. How are you doing in school? Maybe I should ask, "What are you doing in school?" Better yet, for some of you, "Why aren't you in school?" Whatever your situation, you must understand that a good education is your passport to a better future. No matter what you have heard, there is a future for each of you.

Younger girls (10 to 13 years old) need to start thinking about their educational futures. Be mindful of what you are passionate about, your skills, and talents. Girls 14 to 15 need to be planning. And girls 16+ need to be acting on their plans!

So, what plans do you have for your education? I suggest you get serious about this. There is no time like the present. To get started, use the information you listed in the previous section.

GOAL	PLAN TO ACHIEVE IT
Pass my test	Go to all classes, pay attention, take notes, complete homework, and study.
Pass to the next grade	Attend school and pass all my classes.
Graduate from HS	Take all required courses to graduate and pass all my classes.
Go to college (4-year or community)	Start planning in 7th grade with my parents, school counselor, or other concerned adults; prepare for SATs; start looking early for scholarship money and/or work to raise tuition; research different schools of interest; maintain grades; talk to people in careers that interest me and go to work with them.
Go to trade school	Develop my skills, research schools that will train me well, look for scholarship money early and/or work to raise tuition, talk to people in the field.

These are just a few ideas to guide you in preparing your own plan. Adding time frames for these goals, as you did in the previous exercise, will help keep you on track. Never give up on your goals. As situations change in your life, you may need to readjust them.

Rites of Passage - Going from elementary school to middle school, middle school to high school, or high school to college or career can be exciting, confusing, and fearful all at the same time. Here are some tools and tips to help you make the transition a little less painful and a more joy-filled experience as you navigate through the world on your journey to womanhood.

HIGH SCHOOL 101:
Transitioning from Middle School to High School

YAY!!! You've made it to high school - away from the "little girls." Outside of the transition you will make from high school to college (or career if you choose not to go to college), this is one of the most important times of your life. It can also be one of the most overwhelming experiences of your life. There are going to be many things that are different from where you came from. You're going to have to get to know how to get around a new school, you will be making new friends, and you will meet new teachers who are going to expect more of you as they, hopefully, will be working to prepare you for college or your chosen career path. In addition, peer pressure to do drugs, drink alcohol, and have sex usually increases now. Even though it all may sound scary, it's nothing you can't handle with some preparation. Here are some tips and tools, or ***WORDS OF WISDOM***, to make the journey a little easier.

WORD OF WISDOM #1:
Use the Resources Right in Front of You

- Use your teachers, counselors, doctors, parents, clergy, and friends to help you deal with problems.

- Use help hotlines if you aren't comfortable speaking to these people. You can make the call(s) without them knowing who you are.

- High school is going to be a time of changes - most of them should be for the better.

WORD OF WISDOM #2:
Work on Developing Your Self-Worth & Sense of Value

- Be proud of your heritage and represent yourself with a sense of comfort and pride regardless of what others might be doing around you. Over the summer, get to know who you are a little better and why you are proud of your heritage. Read positive books by your favorite female author(s) and/

or watch documentaries about your specific history to boost your pride. Visit the Smithsonian National Museum of African American History & Culture (NMAAHC), and other cultural museums, to expand your history and knowledge and to learn about your unique background. No need to be arrogant about it – just confident. Allow students from other backgrounds to teach you about their heritage as well.

- Strengthen your self-respect and start developing a bottom-line around what you WILL and WILL NOT do or accept before you start high school and as you go through, so that you can STAND for that when you are in a challenging situation.

WORD OF WISDOM #3:
Prepare Yourself for the Ups & Downs of High School

- New independence and new experiences will bring joy but may also bring fears and disappointment – be prepared for all of it.

- Enjoy the fun stuff that's going to happen – going to your first co-ed party (maybe); learning to drive; staying home without a babysitter for the first time; and going to the mall or first date on your own.

- Use **GIGO-II** to help you through the less fun stuff and to help you work on the areas of your life that you are not happy about.

This is the time when you should start learning how to advocate for yourself:

1.   If you are feeling pressure to do something you don't want to do or that you feel is wrong, tell a friend, parent, or counselor to help you find a solution.

2.   If you are not doing well academically, find a tutor or someone to help you.

3.   If you feel socially isolated, try joining a school club or group to make new friends.

4.   Don't let others bully you if you feel different. Tell someone – don't suffer in silence.

Give it time – high school might feel overwhelming at first but, hopefully, things will get better, and you will have a great experience. Check out the resources at the end of this chapter.

COLLEGE 101:
Transitioning from High School to College

My prayer for you is that great things happen in your life as you transition into adulthood. Although for many the step up to college won't be a huge academic difference, what will be different is the atmosphere where learning and studying take place. This can present a huge challenge to some freshmen. If you go away to school, you will experience a level of autonomy that you've never had before - no mom and dad around to tell you what to do. If you are like most girls, you will have the discipline to handle the new college culture without too many bumps - but for some, it can be too much. I wanted to share some valuable tips and tools or, **WORDS OF WISDOM**, to help prepare you for, what I hope will be, the *TIME OF YOUR LIFE!* It was for me .

This transition is a major turning point in your life. Being prepared is critical - whether you go on to a community college, an HBCU (Historically Black College/University), a PWI (Predominately White Institution), or a big or small college or university. Being prepared can be the difference between a successful and enjoyable experience and disappointment and dropping out, or heaven forbid - being put out! Unfortunately, I have found that some girls of color come out of high school not prepared academically or socially for college. In some cases, the education they received was not adequate, or, in other instances, the girls just goofed off during their junior and senior years. I also found, unlike my experience in high school where I had excellent guidance in choosing colleges, many girls of color do not have the guidance they need to make informed decisions during the college selection process including financial aid and housing. These observations aren't the reality for all girls of color - many thrive in high school. My **WORDS OF WISDOM** are meant for all of you.

WORD OF WISDOM #1:
Strengthen Your Academics Over the Summer

- Pre-college summer programs at the school you will be attending can be beneficial, although not the only way you can get prepared. Be mindful that on-campus summer experiences might present issues that you need to be prepared to address – including access to drugs (including "academic doping"), alcohol, and sexual activity as you will be more loosely monitored than at a summer camp. You need to be aware of all these issues anyway.

- Read and write over the summer to keep your skills fresh This is an area that many of my friends who are college professors tell me their students are unprepared for and end up taking non-credit developmental education classes, especially in reading, math, and/or writing.

    1. Practice your outline and note taking skills (VERY important in college)

    2. Strengthen your study skills (also VERY important in college)

    3. If these skills are lacking, do some work over the summer before you get to college! You want to be/stay on track from the beginning, not have to play catch-up, which can affect you mentally and emotionally.

WORD OF WISDOM #2:
Improve Your Life/Social Skills Over the Summer

- Learn and strengthen your self-advocacy skills. You will need them to help you speak up to a professor, your roommate when you disagree, or to get help, whether for academic, health, or social issues.

- Develop and improve your time-management skills – use an alarm clock and calendars or other scheduling devices where you can keep a schedule of classes along with due dates for papers and exams. Getting used to being at least 10-15 minutes early for class or appointments now will help you in the future. Make it a habit now!

WORD OF WISDOM #3:
Develop/Strengthen/Maintain Your Sense of Pride & Self-Worth

- Refer to *WORDS OF WISDOM #2 from HIGH SCHOOL 101: Transitioning from Middle School to High School.*

- Go over the tips given for girls transitioning from Middle School to High School – Strengthen your self-respect and develop a bottom-line around what you WILL and WILL NOT do or accept before you go away, so that you can STAND for that when you are in a challenging situation. Here are a few examples:

    1. Knowing that you won't touch your drink if you've left it unattended to

go dancing or to the restroom and come back/you don't know who might have put something in it;

2. Knowing that you WON'T get in the car with anyone who has been drinking; always carry some "EXTRA" MONEY to get a cab/Uber home;

3. Knowing that you won't cheat on a test or buy a paper just because someone else has the answers or access/not a good idea;

4. Knowing that you are ENOUGH and don't need to get wrapped up in a partner.

Your self-worth and value are very important.

WORD OF WISDOM #4:
Be Sociable & Be Careful

- Get to know students from everywhere, not just the ones that look like you. This is a great way to expose yourself to other cultures, races, and opportunities outside of your comfort zone.

- Attend activities that interest you on a regular basis. Be careful not to become over committed. Learn to balance your schoolwork with your social life. You don't want to flunk out because you were too busy with activities and not spending time on your studies – which is why you are there in the first place.

- Safeguard your physical and mental well-being. When exhausted, rest. Eat proper food and plan exercise into your schedule.

- Take a look at "Tips for First-Year Students" | to read the entire list, go to this link: *-http://www.smu.edu/Provost/ALEC/NeatStuffforNewStudents/ TipsforFirst-YearStudents.*

WORD OF WISDOM #5:
Set & Manage Realistic College Expectations

- Many students have fairytale expectations of college life based on stories from relatives, brochures, and the media. Here is an excerpt, in the form of six questions, from an article that emphasizes the importance of dispelling the freshman myth and instead setting yourself up for reality, success, and fun. Read the entire article here: *http://www.huffingtonpost.com/brian-harke/high-school-to-college-tr_b_620043.html.*

These are great discussion topics for you to have with your parent/guardian.

1. What are your short and long-term goals both academically and personally when you get to college? This means more than getting good grades.

2. How do you think your relationships with your family members will change when you go to college, because they will?

3. Do you expect your college grades to be like those you got in high school? If so, how will you feel if they are not? How will you deal with these feelings and improve?

4. Do you think you will need any outside help to do well in your courses? If not, why? If yes, how will you find it?

5. Will it be difficult to discipline yourself to keep academic commitments, such as attending classes and being prepared for classes? If not, why do you think so? If so, what skills will you need to manage it?

6. Do you think you will feel stressed out at college? If so, list five ways to deal with it. If not, why not? Keep in mind, most students will feel some stress.

BONUS INFO FOR GIRLS – Here are "Five Things Every Black Freshman Girl Needs to Know Before Starting College" by Delece Smith. Cute and so on-point:

1. Bring your walking shoes: Wearing three-inch heels on your first day may sound like a good idea. It may look like a good idea, too – until you realize that your psychology class is father away from your dorm than expected.

2. Search for a good hairdresser – now. It's Friday, your last class has let out, and you're excited to go to the first party of the year. Humidity has turned your "do" into a frizzy mess, and you need to find a hairdresser ASAP. It could be someone on campus.

3. Invest in a purse that poses as a backpack, or vice versa. Everyone wants to look fly on campus, and the right bag elevates an outfit from acceptable to awesome. If it's too cute and too small, it probably can't hold the three-subject notebook you'll need for classes. If it's a big and bulky bag, it will overshadow your new jeans.

4. Avoid the freshman 15, or better yet, the freshman 25 -- pounds. You might think you'll get a good workout walking back and forth to class, up and down all those hills, but you may not. Between late night trips to the dining hall and a new dependency on Ramen noodles, the calories add up, multiply, and cling to your hips. African Americans are leading in obesity trends, with women tipping the scales more than men.

http://www.beyondblackwhite.com/college-girls-guide-getting-school-without-perpetually-clueless-dateless/

http://madamenoire.com/129044/color-on-campus-what-it-really-feels-like-to-be-the-only-black-girl/

http://hechingerreport.org/think-black-boys-face-a-rough-road-to-college-try-being-a-black-girl/

https://www.healthychildren.org/English/ages-stages/young-adult/Pages/The-Transition-from-High-School-to-College.aspx

http://www.smu.edu/Provost/ALEC/NeatStuffforNewStudents/HowIsCollegeDifferentfromHighSchool

http://www.collegeview.com/articles/article/transitioning-from-high-school-to-college-academics

http://www.huffingtonpost.com/brian-harke/high-school-to-college-tr_b_620043.html

http://jezebel.com/college-101-making-the-transition-from-high-school-to-1566703270

http://www.central.edu/parents/advice/making-the-transition/

CAREER 101: Transitioning successfully from High School to a Career or Vocational Training

(https://sdvirtualschools.com/tips-to-successfully-transition-from-high-school-to-a-career/)

In the past, so many young people were encouraged to go to college after high school and then get a career. More and more, young girls who are not interested in college are being encouraged to prepare for a bright future in a career that focuses on their strengths and not feel bad about not going to college. Although I believe college is extremely important – it is not for everyone -- but EDUCATION is!

Some girls know exactly what they want to do and have been working in that space for years before graduating from high school. Others have been struggling and feel that going into the workforce after high school is the better option for them. This transition can be challenging, but here are several tips to help make it a little easier:

1. Get involved in clubs, organizations, and volunteer opportunities.

2. Get some real-world experience.

3. Think about your passions and skills.

4. Take a variety of courses.

5. Start looking for opportunities in the workforce early.

6. Work with the Department of Employment Services in your city/town.

7. Never stop learning – EDUCATION IS FOR EVERYONE!

Here are a few routes to consider:

1. Trade or technical school (beautician/cosmetologist; etc.)

2. Military service

3. Apprenticeship programs (electrician, construction, culinary, etc.)

WORD OF WISDOM #1:
Strengthen Your Skills in Your Area of Interest

What is unique about you? What do you love to do that you think could be translated into a career? Are there skills that people are always asking you for that you might be able to get paid for? Have you had a dream about starting a business, or have you started businesses during your teens? Use the answers to these questions to help you find your place.

6 Tips for Tackling the Transition from College to Career:
(https://www.macslist.org/career-happiness/6-tips-tackling-transition-college-career)

1. Acknowledge that you're in a transition. Be truthful to yourself and others about your situation and its challenges.

2. Create an accountability group. Most young people experience some lulls between college and full-time work.

3. Keep a journal.

4. Master the hard skills (Example: technical knowledge or training).

5. Work on your soft skills (include things like thinking, behavior, and personal traits).

6. Stay current.

WORD OF WISDOM #2:
Be Courageous | Take Risks | Dream BIG

You did it! Be proud of this milestone – graduating from high school and preparing yourself for a productive and purposeful life.

BONUS INFO FOR PARENTS/GUARDIANS – Monitoring College Students From A Distance (for the complete article visit *https://www.healthychildren.org/English/ ages-stages/young-adult/Pages/The-Transition-from-High-School-to-College.aspx)*

•   Short of secretly taking up residence in an adjacent dorm room, what can parents do to keep tabs on a son or daughter living away from home? Dr.

Coleman recommends "the age-old wisdoms: Call regularly, encourage visits home whenever possible and visit your youngster more frequently than just on Parents' Day. Also, if you can, get to know the parents of the roommate or suite mates. If necessary, you can do a little networking together behind the scenes."

- If you suspect that your youngster is having difficulty adapting to college (homesickness, for example, is common among students living away from home for the first time), encourage her to speak to a counselor at the student health service. If you're truly worried about her welfare, make the call yourself and ask one of the mental-health professionals there to pay a visit to your youngster or invite her down to talk.

WHO IS GOING TO PAY YOUR BILLS?
$$ Financial Goals $$

You are, that's who! You have everything you need to prosper. You don't have to have a million dollars to live a quality life. You need a plan for your financial future, so you can live comfortably with what you have. If you want a lot of money, you certainly need a plan to make that happen.

Do you want to buy clothes, the latest version of iPhone, go to college or trade school, and purchase a car or a home someday? You may be able to have someone else pay for it now, but you must learn the value of being able to pay for it yourself. As a little girl, I was taught to save my money for extra things I wanted. I worked around the house for extra money and felt good when I bought something. Providing services or making something to sell can be a way to help you raise money for the things you want on your way to starting/owning your own business - being an entrepreneur. ***OPERATION HOPE and THE WEALTH FACTORY, Inc.***, our financial literacy partners, are great resources that teach young people about banking and business - *www.operationhope.org and www.getwealthylife.com.*

Today, many girls are given anything they want from adults and sometimes boys or girls. Money doesn't grow on trees and people don't always have it to give, so I encourage you to develop a healthy respect for it. Respect for money means that you recognize the struggle in working for it and you pay more attention to how it is spent. Rather than stressing over what you don't have, learn to be grateful for what you do have. This is sometimes easier said than done.

Okay, let's keep this simple. What do you want that will cost money? Using the "**My Personal Goals**" chart you already filled out at the beginning of the section will come in handy.

GOAL	PLAN TO ACHIEVE IT
A new iPad ($399.00)	Save my allowance (if you get one), or money from a job.
A new flat screen TV ($150 - $400+)	Ask my parents for half, and work for the balance.
Go to college-$9,000/year to $50,000+/year	Look for scholarship money, use as many resources as I can, school loan, ask my parents, get a job, and save money.
Buy a condo/home-$250,000+, or rent an apartment	Establish good credit, pay bills on time, streamline spending, and set an amount to save each month.

These are just a few goals you might have, depending on your age and circumstances. If you have not already added to your personal list, take time to do that now.

$$ Suggestions $$

1. Save your allowance, money you receive from working, or gifts. This is the first step in your financial planning. Save for what you want and keep the rest until you need it.

2. Open a savings account. Ask an adult to help you do this. It is important that you become familiar with banks and the way they operate. Regularly depositing or withdrawing your money is a good way to help you understand the process. Watching your money grow builds great self-esteem.

3. Learn about and purchase stocks and real estate. This is one of the true gateways to wealth. There are a lot of young people trading on the Stock Exchange and learning about real estate. You can join them. Find a knowledgeable adult to guide you. There are junior investment clubs and other resources where you can get additional information about both.

Bottom line:

"Want what you have so that someday you can have what you want."

Financial planning can make the difference between a life filled with stress and a future filled with prosperity.

WHAT DO YOU WANT TO BE WHEN YOU GROW UP?

Career Goals

You need to set career goals, whether you plan to go to college or not. Perhaps you have not been able to finish high school; you still need to be thinking about a career.

Whatever your circumstances, try to visualize your life in ten years. What do you hope to be doing?

What do you enjoy doing? It's wonderful knowing what you are good at and having others' acknowledgment, encouragement, and support. Everyone has a special gift that the world is waiting to experience. Determining and developing those strengths can be exciting and sometimes frustrating. Try to keep an open mind. Remember, there is only one of you, and only you can fulfill your Creator's mission.

Let's slow the pace a little and try to determine your natural talents and/or other areas of interest.

A. What makes you unique? List some of your special talents/interests:

1. _____   5. _____

2. _____   6. _____

3. _____   7. _____

4. _____   8. _____

B. Some ways to determine your natural talents:

1. Participate in school and/or church activities.

2. Run for a school office. It might lead to a leadership or political career.

3. Volunteer outside of school.

4. Develop your hobbies.

5. Spend time with people who do interesting things.

C. Developing your interests:

1. Become active in school clubs.

2. Seek membership in groups outside of school.

3. Take on leadership roles.

4. Attend a school specifically geared toward your interests:

   - Duke Ellington School of the Arts (Washington, DC)

   - Fashion Institute of Technology (New York City, NY)

   - Cosmetology School

   - Carpentry, Electrical, Computer, Culinary, etc.

5. Find a mentor - someone in the field that interests you.

Once you have an idea of the area you would like to pursue, it's time to start planning. You can begin setting goals for your career.

GOAL	PLAN TO ACHIEVE IT
To be in a helping profession.	Help with my younger sister or brother and start volunteering
To work until age 55+.	Develop a good work ethic: be on time, perform well, stay healthy, and dress and behave appropriately
Be a teacher, singer, IT professional, chef, or doctor.	Meet people in the profession, learn the educational requirements, start saving, and research financial aid resources
To own my own business.	Meet some business owners, read about starting a business, maintain good grades.

Now that you have gone through these exercises, I hope you have a better idea about the importance of planning for your future. Your future is what you make it. Don't be discouraged if you have no clue about what you want to do or become. With the guidance of caring adults, and this book, I guarantee that you will get closer to discovering your purpose. Enjoy the journey as you find it.

TO ACHIEVE YOUR DREAMS
REMEMBER YOUR ABC's

Avoid negative sources, people, places, things, and habits.

Believe in yourself.

Consider things from every angle.

Don't give up and don't give in.

Enjoy life today; yesterday is gone and tomorrow may never come.

Family and friends are hidden treasures. Seek them and enjoy their richness.

Give more than you planned to give.

Hang on to your dreams.

Ignore those who try to discourage you.

Just do it!

Keep on trying. No matter how hard it seems, it will get easier.

Love yourself, first and foremost.

Make it happen.

Never lie, cheat, or steal. Always strike a fair deal.

Open your eyes and see things as they are.

Practice makes perfect!

Quitters never win and winners never quit.

Read, study, and learn about everything important in your life.

STOP PROCRASTINATING!

Take control of your destiny.

Understand yourself to better understand others.

Visualize it.

Want it more than anything.

X-ray yourself before x-raying others.

You are God's unique creation. Nothing can replace you.

Zero in on your target and go for it.

"LOVE YOURSELF! HONOR YOURSELF! RESPECT YOURSELF!"

A PAGE FOR YOUR POSITIVE THOUGHTS
(END OF CHAPTER CHECK-IN!)

CONVERSATIONS WITH HOPE, LOVE, AND GRACE

So I'm working on having better relationships with adults, especially the police. I'm learning to respect adult authority and getting them to listen to me. Who would have thought a little respect goes a long way!?!

Check out the 10 COMMANDMENTS OF HOW TO GET ALONG WITH PEOPLE at the end of this chapter. We MUST do better!

I've got to learn how to resolve conflicts better. I really need to read this chapter!

"I attract happy, healthy and whole people, because I am happy, healthy and whole."

Standard of Excellence #6

Healthy Relationships/ Healthy Communication

Getting Along with Others

(Symbol of justice, fair play, unity, harmony, and avoidance of conflicts)

OPENING EXERCISE

Find someone who does not look like you: a peer, an adult, a person of a different race, or a mentally or physically challenged youth. Talk to him or her about your differences, as well as what you have in common. Use this space to write your responses.

Differences

1. ....

2. ....

3. ....

Similarities

1. ....

2. ....

3. ....

What did you learn about each other?

....

....

....

....

....

....

....

HEALTHY RELATIONSHIPS/ HEALTHY COMMUNICATION

As a young girl, you have probably already developed healthy and unhealthy relationships. Healthy relationships encourage growth and individuality. They are based on mutual respect and acceptance. Unhealthy relationships are restrictive and abusive. They are based on selfishness and fear. If you want to have happy, healthy, and whole relationships, YOU must be happy, healthy, and whole. You attract what you are.

Everyone does not deserve a front row seat in the theater of your life. Only a select few should get that privilege. Most should take their seats in the main area. Others belong in the balcony - you need to keep your distance from them. Still others belong outside in the lobby. Then, there are those who don't even belong in the theater; they should not even be in your life. Determining where people fit in your life takes time. You may not have too much say about some people. However, it is still important to develop a good sense for healthy relationships and the ability to communicate with all types of people.

This chapter includes feedback from girls, boys, and adults and some information about how to get along with people, including people who don't look like you.

CHARACTERISTICS OF HEALTHY RELATIONSHIPS

What is a relationship? Very simply, a relationship is some type of connection with someone. It could be with family members, your girlfriends, boys, adults in school, or people you meet in general. Some are closer than others. It all depends on the connection. No matter what the connection, there are common traits in all healthy relationships. How would you rate your relationships?

Ingredients for a healthy, non-abusive relationship:

RESPECT

- Listening without judging

- Being emotionally supportive and understanding

- Valuing opinions

TRUST AND SUPPORT

- Supporting goals

- Respecting a person's right to their feelings, friends, activities, decisions, and opinions, regardless of whether you agree

- Sharing common interests and activities

- Experiencing mutual happiness

HONESTY AND ACCOUNTABILITY

- Accepting responsibility for self

- Acknowledging past mistakes

- Admitting when you are wrong

- Communicating openly and truthfully, without trying to manipulate the other person or situation

NEGOTIATION AND FAIRNESS

- Seeking mutually satisfying resolutions to conflict

- Accepting change

- Being willing to compromise

- Working together

So, how did you do? The better you know, love, and respect yourself, the more likely you will want to be in healthy relationships.

What do you do when you have unhealthy relationships? First, look at yourself. Do you exhibit the traits you just read about? If not, try to improve and work at a better understanding of yourself. If other people are not acting in healthy ways, you may need to distance yourself from them. If it is impossible to do that, try talking to a supportive, trustworthy adult. When the situation is very unhealthy, and perhaps dangerous, get help from a counselor or trusted adult who can help you find a healthier environment.

TIPS FOR HEALTHY YOUTH-ADULT RELATIONSHIPS:

Youth – Parent or Guardian: Healthy relationships with your parents or guardians means that they are adjusting to your changing needs as you grow from child to tween and tween to teen. You want them to:

- Be supportive. You want them to guide not dictate.

- Be patient and available. You might not always take their advice the first time, but when you are ready, you want them to be in your corner; you also want to be able to take that same advice from someone else – it happens to me all the time – without them getting mad. Sometimes you can only "hear" it from someone else.

- Be open. You want them to listen with non-judgmental ears.

- Be understanding. You want to be able to learn from your failures and mistakes while still being supported and loved.

- Be empathetic. You don't want them to make fun of or minimize your feelings.

Goal – Provide girls with a sense of safety, security, and trust; a sense of belonging; and the ability to deal with stress.

Youth – Teacher: Healthy relationships with teachers and other adults in leadership positions means that there is an advocate for you who understands your interests, struggles, and ambitions. It also means that they are appropriate with you whenever you are communicating with them. What can happen when you have a positive relationship with your teacher(s):

- Helps you feel like you belong to the school community.

- Feelings of belonging can help increase your motivation, your social behavior, and your academic achievement.

- Provides a safe place if your primary caregiver is not healthy themselves.

Goal – Provide girls with a connection to their school community and a sense that their teachers genuinely care, believe in them, and are interested in their success.

Youth – Police: Healthy relationships with the police and other authority figures means understanding and mutual respect between both parties and striving for quality interaction, police learning about youth development and the lives of girls/youth that they encounter, and girls/youth learning about the law and their rights. Here are some results of good relationships between girls/youth and the police:

- Improved relations between teens, the police, and the community.

- Reduced complaints, confrontations, and arrests for minor offenses, as well as improved mixing of police with community programming and resources.

• Officers with youth training have reduced job stress, which can lead to fewer conflicts getting out of hand.

Goal – *Police departments that learn about and respect the communities they work in and communities that get to know and respect the police that serve their community. Youth developing respect for the law and the peacekeepers in their community, while also engaging with law enforcement in meaningful ways.*

Relationship Resources:

Parent Toolkit - http://www.ontariodirectors.ca/pe_images/Code_ParentToolKit_ENG.pdf
Strategies for Youth - http://strategiesforyouth.org/

"A loving relationship cannot exist without communication. Research shows that kids believe they have valuable things to say. When parents or guardians ask their children, and listen genuinely, it helps build self-esteem and confidence."

- Office of National Drug Control Policy/Partnership for a Drug-Free America

A healthy relationship is empowering, not limiting. It involves sharing ideas, listening without judging, being honest, and being sensitive.

I asked different people about healthy relationships and communication. Below are their responses. These are a mixture of responses between 2000 & 2020:

"I treat people the way I want to be treated."
—**Elizabeth Ferebee (my Mom, deceased)**

"Listen to your parents and respect your elders."
—**Elliot Ferebee (my Dad, deceased)**

"I do not allow anyone to challenge me in a negative manner. When things are going well, and I have so much to be thankful for, someone may test me anticipating a negative reaction. Through faith and belief in God, I know I have been blessed and know that God has the solution."
—**Lynnette Banks (Former youth in the Washington Area Project for Youth - Youth at Risk Program and former Got It Goin' On® Empowerment Program - Assistant Director, Washington, D.C. Now a mother of two daughters)**

"A healthy relationship is nourishment to the human anatomy."
—**Anika Williams-Brewer | CEO of S.A.F.E. House (Saving A Family Early) & Author of BEAUTY IN A DESERT PLACE**

"When it comes to communicating, we should listen to respond, not to react."
—**LeTonya F. Moore, Esq., Brand Protection Practitioner™**

"Healthy communication is interacting with others, getting to know them better, sharing your beliefs, and just showing them that you love them. By making them feel good, you feel good about yourself."
—Donavan J. Lee (Former Member of Metropolitan Baptist Church Teen Ministry, Washington, D.C.)

"Be yourself...everyone else is taken."
—Jamie Brannon, 14-years old from Rhode Island

"I think the key to healthy communication in any relationship is to always be blunt and completely honest about one's feelings. I think that the worst thing to do is to sugar coat one's attitude toward a situation to spare the other party's feelings. Although respect should be shown all the time, I feel that one should say what is on his/her mind and heart. This openness eliminates confusion and contempt and allows for productive problem-solving conversations."
—Shani A. Lee (Former Member of Metropolitan Baptist Church Teen Ministry, Washington, D.C.)

"I am surrounded by a lot of different kinds of people because I attend a public school. I don't treat anyone different from anyone else. I speak to anyone who comes my way or into my space. I give respect to people because that is how I wish to be treated. To have a healthy relationship involves a lot of things such as trust, respect, and being able to talk to one another when you need help with problems or different situations. There must also be someone who you can talk to and feel comfortable with, which for me is GOD. Then you can learn how to grow through your problems and use them to make your relationship much stronger."
—Mysha Johnson (Former Member of Metropolitan Baptist Church Teen Ministry, Washington, D.C.)

"The key to communication is first - to be honest, second - to be honest, and last but not least -to be HONEST!"
—Tineal Summers (Former Washington Area Project for Youth Mentee; Former Got It Goin' On® Empowerment Program – Assistant Director, Washington, D.C.; and member of Alpha Kappa Alpha Sorority, Inc.)

"If something feels wrong, follow the feeling and explore. People tend to let you know who they are in small pieces. Trust your inner thermostat and press pause for a minute. Those feelings are rarely ever wrong."
—Marcelle Applewhaite, RN, MSN (Childhood friend from Westbury, Long Island, New York)

Everyone has his or her own way of communicating. Be sure that you first learn to love and respect yourself, so you can communicate with others in a loving and respectful way, no matter who they are and what they look like. If you can do that, your relationships will also be loving and respectful.

- You can be respectful and loving to a perfect stranger by acknowledging his or her presence.

- You can be loving and respectful to an abusive relative by "loving them from a distance."

- You can overcome hatred of an entire race of people by researching their history, and getting to know individuals of that race. This will allow you to develop tolerance and understanding for others, just as you would want yourself.

THE TEN COMMANDMENTS OF HOW TO GET ALONG WITH PEOPLE

1. Keep chains on your tongue. Always say less than you think. Cultivate a low persuasive voice. How you say it often counts more than what you say.

2. Make promises sparingly, and keep them faithfully, no matter what they cost.

3. Never let an opportunity pass to say a kind and encouraging word to or about someone. Praise good work regardless of who did it.

4. Be interested in others - their pursuits, their work, their homes, and their families. Let everyone you meet, however humble, feel that you regard him or her as a person of importance.

5. Be cheerful; don't depress or burden those around you by dwelling on your aches and pains and small disappointments. Remember that everyone is carrying some type of burden.

6. Keep an open mind. Discuss, but don't argue. It is a mark of a superior mind to be able to disagree without being disagreeable.

7. Let your virtues, if you have any, speak for themselves. Refuse to talk about the vices of others. Discourage gossip. It's a waste of valuable time and can be destructive and hurtful.

8. Take into consideration the feelings of others. Wit and humor at the expense of another is never worth the pain that may be inflicted.

9. Pay no attention to ill-natured remarks about you. Remember the person who carried the message may not be the most accurate reporter in the world. Simply live so that nobody will believe them.

10. Don't be anxious about the credit due you. Do your best and be patient. Forget about yourself and let others "REMEMBER." Success is much sweeter that way.

(Found on the Teachers' Bulletin Board at Park View Elementary School, Washington, DC)

A PAGE FOR YOUR POSITIVE THOUGHTS

(END OF CHAPTER CHECK-IN!)

CONVERSATIONS WITH LOVE, HOPE, FAITH, GRACE, CHARITY, PEACE, AND JOY

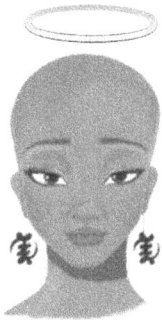

You know they call us Generation Z! We are adopters, influencers, smart, independent, media-minded, sophisticated, visual, and focused on our futures.

I can use the etiquette skills in this chapter in my new cooking business and teach other young people what to do. There is so much I need to learn.

You know, etiquette is more than just what knife & fork to use. It also includes common courtesy & food manners, I am learning how to have a positive place in society.

It's time to learn about giving back and making a difference. There are many powerful role models to follow after.

I think it's important to advocate for girls in the US & other parts of the world who don't have access to quality education.

There are so many causes to speak up about. I want to attend a protest or rally for a cause I believe in. What are some of the causes you believe in?

Let's empower all girls to find their positive place in the world, help others when we can, and help raise money so others can live better lives.

"I am thankful for people older than me, who take time to teach me the right thing."

Standard of Excellence #7

....

A Positive Place In Society
Social Skills for Generation Z & Generation Alpha
Philanthropy & Giving Back Advocacy & Social Justice

(Symbol of patience, self-containment, self-discipline, and self-control)

A POSITIVE PLACE IN SOCIETY
Doing the Right Thing

There are no second chances to make a good first impression! You may get another chance, but the first impression will have already been made. Go through life with your best foot forward, looking YOUR best on the outside, feeling good on the inside, and acting kind and respectful towards yourself and others. That's what makes a good impression.

Proper social skills can include common courtesy, common sense, good manners, and thoughtfulness. Adults call this etiquette. To have a positive place in society, we must know how to act. I don't mean you must watch your every move or that everyone must act the same way. Individuality is a wonderful thing, but we need to have some sense of what works and what doesn't. Having a positive place in society will depend greatly on your development into a positive person. Use the information you are about to read as a general guideline.

ETIQUETTE FOR GENERATION Z & ALPHA

Relating to others and showing consideration begins at home. Different environments require different behavior, but you must, generally, know how to act.

Let's play **21st CENTURY ETIQUETTE**, a game to help girls handle social situations. The categories are: *"At Home," "At School and In Public,"* and *"In Business or Volunteering."*

"AT HOME"	
QUESTION	ANSWER
1. What is the best way to treat the adults in your home?	Respect your elders. Watch them through loving eyes. They have much to teach you. Treat them with respect.
2. How can your parents/guardians understand anything about your life?	Let them into your world, including inviting them into your social media life. This builds bridges to stronger relationships that may prove beneficial to you in the future.

You may think they are too old and out of it, but they care about you and want to guide you. Talk with them about yourself. If there are adults with whom you do not feel safe, share your concerns with a trustworthy adult.

1. What can you do to give your home a more pleasant atmosphere?	Cooperate and help around the house. Clean up after yourself. You aren't the only one who occupies that space.
2. How can you show respect on phone calls?	Learn proper phone etiquette.
3. How can you be respectful using your cell phone or other electronic devices at home?	Turn them off when sharing time with family.

Learn how to balance your time on devices so that you don't become addicted to them. Spend quality time with family and friends or engaging in interesting activities AWAY from your device.

In SCHOOL and in PUBLIC	
QUESTION	ANSWER
1. How do you earn a good reputation?	Hang out with positive people. Carry yourself with respect.

People judge you by the types of friends you hang out with. You are who you hang with.

2. How do you respect the privacy of others?	Mind your own business!

If it's not about you, don't get in it. The only exception would be circumstances where you are trying to help someone - like, if you see someone being bullied, or you know of someone being abused. Speak up if you feel confident enough, and/or get a responsible adult immediately if you feel you would be in danger.

3. How should you speak to others?	Speak clearly, without using foul or inappropriate language.

When you are with friends, you should feel comfortable using familiar language, but keep it respectful. Calling each other the "b" word or the "n" word is not respectful. With adults, speak clearly and confidently, so they can understand you.

4. What is proper internet & Zoom etiquette?	No yelling (ALL CAPS), don't use sarcasm, think before you type, show up in decent attire, and be kind and appropriate.
5. How can you become a better person?	Be kind and considerate to yourself and others. Respect adults. Don't disrespect people.

Offer a kind word or do a kind deed for someone. Say "Please," "Thank You," or "Excuse Me" when it's appropriate. Don't talk loudly or use foul language while in public places. Don't talk back to adults - that's rude.

6. What is one area that many young people have trouble with when they eat?	Proper table manners. See next page.

Whether at home or in public, act like a young lady and use manners.

TABLE MANNERS

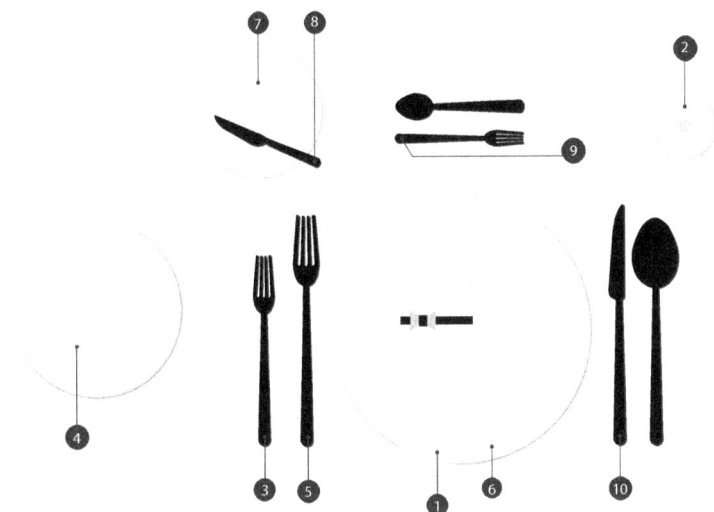

DO

Put your napkin **(#1)** in your lap as soon as you sit down.

Unless the hostess tells you to go ahead, wait until everyone at the table is seated before you start eating.

Use the salad fork **(#3)** with your salad. Place your fork across your salad plate **(#4)** when finished.

Take one roll or slice of bread and place on bread/butter plate **(#7)**.

Use your butter knife **(#8)** for your roll or slice of bread.

Break off a small piece of bread/roll, butter it and eat it. Continue to do this until all the bread/roll is gone.

If you must, excuse yourself when you need to leave the table. Put napkin back on your lap when you return.

Put knife and fork across your plate when you are finished eating.

Tell your hostess "Thank You" before leaving.

DON'T!

Use someone else's glass. Your glass is in the upper right corner **(#2)**

Pick up utensils with hands in fist position. Place utensils between your fingers.

Use the salad fork **(#3)** for your main meal. Use the larger fork **(#5)** next to your main plate **(#6).**

Use your dinner knife **(#10)** for the butter.

Put butter on the entire roll or slice of bread and put it in your mouth.

Talk with food in your mouth. Only cut and place bite-size portions in your mouth. Don't stuff your face.

Use your dinner utensils for dessert. Use the dessert spoon or fork **(#9)** above the plate. They are sometimes brought to you when dessert is served.

"LIFE IN GENERAL"

1. What is one way to earn respect?

If you talk the talk, make sure you can walk the walk.

Mean what you say and say what you mean. Being young is no excuse for irresponsible behavior!

2. What is one tool that will sharpen your mind?

Reading and staying informed about current events.

Reading is an awesome gift that everyone should take advantage of. Read everything that is educational, entertaining, or inspirational. Make sure it is appropriate; there's a lot of trash out there.

3. What can you do for someone who has helped you?

Let them know you appreciate them by saying or doing something nice for them.

When someone does something that you appreciate, let him or her know. Say, "Thank you."

Send a note, make a phone call, e-mail them, or thank them in person. Don't take their kindness for granted.

"PHILANTHROPY & GIVING BACK TO THE COMMUNITY"

WHAT IS IT & WHAT DOES IT MEAN TO YOU?

PHILANTHROPY – 1. Goodwill to other people; active effort to promote human welfare. 2. An act or gift done or made for humanitarian purposes. Giving of your time, talent, or tithes (money) to benefit others or a cause.

Words you might also hear that mean the same thing: benevolence, generosity, humanitarianism, public-spiritedness, altruism, social conscience, charity, brotherly love, unselfishness, humanity, kindness, and compassion.

Philanthropy and giving back can help build a girl's confidence while helping someone else. It's what many communities of color are built on. Take pride in becoming unselfish and thinking about what you can do for others as you continue your journey to womanhood.

Here are a few historical facts about philanthropy in the African American community as well as women in general and why it's important for girls of color to learn about giving back:

African American Women and Philanthropy

African American women were helpful in assisting runaway slaves, educating other women, forming social organizations, and advocating for civil rights. Had it not been for their strong philanthropic efforts, many social movements may not have been as powerful and lasting, much like Black Lives Matter (Learning to Give).

Women and Philanthropy

Although women have traditionally been volunteers, they have not been widely recognized as philanthropic donors until recently. Increased wealth among women has resulted in a recent surge of committed women philanthropists who are fulfilling their desire for involvement and change (Learning to Give).

African American Sororities

Born at a time in history when the traditional roles of women were being challenged, the founders of the first Black sororities had to overcome the stereotypical views of sexism and racism as well. Now, over three-quarters of a million women belong to Black sororities with numbers increasing annually. These women make a lifetime commitment to continue the legacy of building social capital and upholding the strong ideals of education, integrity, public service, and activism (Learning to Give).

Here are several powerful examples of women of color and philanthropy:

Harriet Tubman: The giving of time and talent during her heroic involvement with the Underground Railroad and fighting against the injustices of slavery.

Rosa Parks: The birth of the modern Civil Rights Movement is shown through the story of Rosa Parks' bravery and determination.

Simone Biles: The idea of philanthropy as giving of your talents (sports accomplishments) is clearly shown through this amazing woman's story.

Oprah Winfrey: Oprah has used her celebrity and her fortune to support various causes, especially toward providing a better education for girls around the world.

Oseola McCarty: Ms. McCarty was a local washerwoman in Hattiesburg, Mississippi, who became the University of Southern Mississippi's most famous contributor. She drew global attention after it was announced in July 1995 that she had established a trust through which, at her death, a portion of her life's savings would be left to the university to provide scholarships for deserving students in need of financial assistance. The amount was estimated at $150,000, a surprising amount given her menial occupation.

Madame C.J. Walker (Sarah Breedlove): Walker is a great example of philanthropy being a diverse American tradition. She was a successful African American businesswoman who supported many causes with the profits of her business. She was the first female self-made millionaire in the US.

As you see, philanthropy can take on various forms. Figure out what is important to you and find ways to make a difference in your community. Being a part of our global society allows you the opportunity to give back to other girls/people around the world. You can volunteer, help raise money, or learn about advocacy.

- Collect clothes and food for the homeless.
- Collect books and school supplies for children in need in the US and/or other countries.
- Walk to raise funds for: Homeless, Health Issues (Cancer, Diabetes, Sickle-Cell Anemia, etc. or Dating & Domestic Violence).

List some of the areas where you would like to make a difference:

1. ....

2. ....

3. ....

Philanthropy Resources:

Learning to Give – www.learningtogive.org

Youth in Philanthropy – www.candid.org

ADVOCACY & SOCIAL JUSTICE

WHAT IS IT & WHAT DOES IT MEAN TO YOU?

The word **advocacy** has its origins in law and is defined in most dictionaries as – the process of speaking on behalf of someone or a cause.

Social justice is defined as – promoting a just society by challenging injustice and valuing diversity.

Most people think of the notion of equality or equal opportunity in society when they think about social justice.

Unfortunately, we live in a world where there are many places where inequalities and injustices exist.

I've listed four issues of inequality below. Add to the list:

1. African American sororities were founded because Black women were not welcome in White sororities. They were able to use their numbers to advocate for causes that were important to them.

2. Girls in some parts of the world do not have equal access to education; some risk their lives to get an education.

3. Example of a young female advocate/activist is Malala Yousafzai, who was born in 1997. She is a Pakistani who is an activist for female education and the youngest-ever Nobel Peace Prize winner. She was shot by the Taliban when she stood up for girls' education. She survived and is still fighting!

4. News coverage of missing young Black girls is slim compared to coverage for missing young white girls.

5. Latino children being "caged" at the Mexico/US border.

6. ....

7. ....

How can you learn to advocate for an issue that's important to you and/or when you see an injustice happening to someone, or in your community? Here are some steps:

Become grounded in who you are – develop confidence in yourself, develop a sense of pride and value, and develop respect for yourself and others.

Develop good writing and speaking skills – Learning how to present yourself on paper and orally (public speaking) will help you to share your ideas more clearly. You will become more comfortable talking to adults and your peers about the things that really make you mad.

Learn the facts about the issue(s) that you want to do something about – Research the issue, talk to individuals who are affected and find out how they feel and what would help them, and attend events with other people who care about this issue and see what they are doing about it.

Get advocacy training that is focused on training for youth – This will help you learn about the different ways to make your voice heard. There is power in numbers – get some of your friends to take this journey with you and encourage them to do the first 3 steps as well!

Get involved in a way that makes sense for you and is safe – Stay close to responsible adults, and don't share your personal information.

Advocacy & Social Justice Resources:

Let Girls Lead – http://www.letgirlslead.org/resources/guide-to-advocacy

The Top 10 List You Don't Want to Be On: Dangerous Places for Girls' Education – http://www.brookings.edu/blogs/education-plus-development/posts/2014/09/23-dangerous-places-girls-education-winthrop-mcgivney

Book – I Am Malala: The Girl Who Stood Up for Education and Was Shot by the Taliban

No One Misses the Missing Black Girls – http://madamenoire.com/79158/no-one-misses-the-missing-black-girls/

Black and Missing Foundation – www.blackandmissinginc.com

A PAGE FOR YOUR POSITIVE THOUGHTS
(END OF CHAPTER CHECK-IN!)

CONVERSATIONS WITH HOPE, PEACE, & CHARITY

I know a bunch of teens that use drugs - some who even overdosed and died. I also have some relatives who are in recovery and they tell me their stories. I don't want any part of it!

My family is dealing with physical abuse, drugs, alcohol and now gambling. There are so many ways to get off track, but my dating violence blog helps to keep me grounded.

One of my mentors told our group that we should embrace our bodies as instruments of beauty, not objects to be taken advantage of. I think thats a good way to show respect for yourself and your body.

"I am valuable and respect myself. I stay away from negative people, places and things. I deserve a happy, healthy, and safe home, community, country, & world!"

❖ ❖ ❖ ❖ ❖ ❖ ❖ ❖ ❖ ❖

Standard of Excellence #8

....

Staying Out Of Harm's Way
Saying NO to Destructive Behavior
(Drugs, Gambling, Violence, and Early Sexual Activity)
& YES, to LIFE!

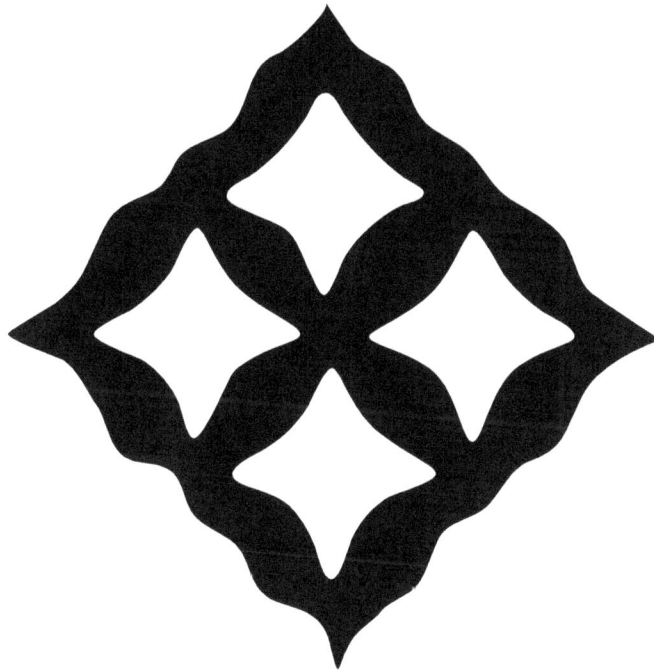

(Symbol of safety, security and love)

OPENING EXERCISE

How much do you know? Here are a few questions to test your knowledge.
The correct answers are at the bottom of the page (Don't look yet!).

1. Is there a cure for AIDS?   Y   N

2. Can alcohol abuse have lasting physical effects?   Y   N

3. Can sexually transmitted diseases have life-long effects?   Y   N

4. Should you tell someone about a friend who may be in
    trouble with drugs, alcohol, or in an abusive relationship?   Y   N

5. If a friend or partner hits you, should you still want them to
    be your friend or partner?   Y   N

6. At a party, should you leave your drink unattended?   Y   N

7. Can gambling become a problem that affects an individual,
    family, and friends?   Y   N

8. What is K2/Spice? ....

9. Can you get cancer from second-hand smoke?   Y   N

10. Should you follow the crowd if everyone is doing drugs?   Y   N

11. Should you get in the car with anyone who has been
    drinking?   Y   N

                                                                                   Y   N
12. Should you share your personal information online?

13. Are there sexual predators and other dangerous people on   Y   N
    the Internet?

Answers: 1) N; 2 Y; 3) Y; 4) Y; 5) N; 6) N; 7) Y; 8) Synthetic Marijuana; 9) Y; 10) N; 11) N; 12) N; 13) Y

STAYING OUT OF HARM'S WAY
"What Part of NO Don't You Understand?!"

Girls often face challenges which threaten to derail their futures. Issues that include:

- Loneliness and boredom
- Violence
- Teenage pregnancy
- Low academic achievement
- Mental, physical, or sexual abuse
- Substance abuse and gambling
- Depression and suicide
- Inappropriate and harmful online behavior
- Negative peer pressure
- Lack of spiritual guidance

Just Saying NO isn't enough anymore. It takes a heavy dose of self-esteem, self-respect, self-knowledge, and self-discipline to keep you from giving in to popular, destructive behaviors.

Reasons girls give for engaging in negative activities:

"I'm bored and the vaping and alcohol social media ads make it look so good."

"He said if I didn't have sex with him, he would find someone else."

"She looked at me the wrong way, so I had to hit her."

"Life at my house is terrible. My parents fight all the time and they don't pay any attention to me. I just needed a way to cope."

"My parents think I'm supposed to be perfect. I can't stand the pressure."

"The Real Housewives ALL yell, curse, and fight all the time and they are getting paid. Why can't I do the same thing?"

For those of you who are about the business of healthy living and developing a strong foundation for life, read this chapter. I pray that you remain positively focused. For those of you whose lives are more challenging, please pay special attention to this chapter. I pray that you have the strength and courage to reach out for help and accept it from someone who extends a hand.

YOU DO HAVE A CHOICE!

This chapter discusses the following self-destructive issues:

- Drugs & Gambling

- Alcohol, Tobacco & Vaping

- Violence (including teen dating violence), Hatred, & Racism

- Early Sexual Activity

THE BOTTOM LINE!

1. Drugs are illegal and can be deadly unless they are prescribed for you and taken responsibly.

2. Alcohol is illegal for juveniles and can also be deadly.

3. Violence, hatred, and racism are unacceptable, ignorant, and can be deadly.

4. Early sexual activity (before you are ready) destroys the purpose for which this wonderful expression of love was created. It can also be deadly!

DRUGS DESTROY DREAMS!

YOUR LIFE IS WORTH LIVING

Sometimes it's hard for adults to talk to young people about alcohol, tobacco, vaping, and drug abuse.

Here are some statistics along with some information that might help:

STATISTICS

- Tobacco use disproportionately affects racial ethnic minorities due to targeted advertising and marketing from the tobacco industry (Report – Truth Initiative Inspiring Tobacco Free Lives | 2014-17).

- In 2018, the US Surgeon General declared that e-cigarettes had reached epidemic proportions among youth, sparked by a 78% increase of use among high school students over a one-year time-period.

- In 2017, approximately 4% of the American adolescent population age 12 to 17 suffered from a substance use disorder; this equals 992,000 teens or 1 in 25 people in this age group (Substance Abuse & Mental Health Services Administration | 2018).

- About 443,000 adolescents ages 12 to 17 had an alcohol use disorder in 2017, or 1.8% of adolescents (Substance Abuse & Mental Health Services Administration | 2018).

- Teenagers and those with mental health disorders are more at risk for drug use and addiction than other populations (National Institute on Drug Abuse | 2018).

DRUG CHARACTERISTICS

For this discussion, we will be talking about illegal drugs, which include alcohol, cigarettes, and vaping.

Drugs prescribed for you by your doctor and over-the-counter medication, when used properly, can promote health. If abused, they can cause addiction, illness, or death. Use of drugs prescribed for others can be harmful to your health.

- *Drugs include any substances that change your mood, chemically alter your brain, or negatively affect bodily functions. They can cause addiction and/or death from first-time or continued use*

Types of drugs:

Stimulants: *Raise blood pressure and speed up the heart rate. Some examples include:*

- Ecstasy

- Speed
- Base
- Ice
- Methamphetamine
- Amphetamine
- Dexamphetamine
- Phentermine
- Methylamphetamine
- Crystal Methylamphetamine
- Para-methoxyamphetamine
- Cocaine
- Crack Cocaine

Hallucinogens: *Produce hallucinations (seeing things that are not there) and paranoid thinking. Some examples include:*

- LSD
- Magic Mushrooms (Psilocybin)
- PCP (Phencyclidine)
- Ketamine
- Mescaline

Depressants: *Depress respiratory system, slow the heart rate, and produce irregular heartbeat and blood pressure. Some examples include:*

- Cannabis (marijuana)
- GHB
- Inhalants
- Heroin
- Morphine
- Codeine
- Methadone
- Buprenorphine
- Pethidine
- Dilaudid
- Kapanol
- MS Contin

- Lean (Purple Drank or Sizzurp)

Inhalants: *Can cause death and severe damage to brain and nervous system; ordinary household products that are inhaled or sniffed.*

Steroids: *Illegal use - Increase body weight and muscular strength.*

Tobacco & Vaping: *Nicotine is both a stimulant and a sedative to the central nervous system; it is highly addictive.*

Alcohol: *Most widely used drug among teenagers! Impairs judgment and coordination.*

DRUGS POPULAR WITH TEENS ALONG WITH STREET NAMES

- Alcohol - Booze, Brew, Liquor

- Anabolic Steroids - Roids, Juice

- Bath Salts - Bloom, Cloud Nine, Vanilla, Sky, White Lightening

- Cocaine - Coke, C, Snow, Flake, Blow, Bump, Candy, Charlie, Rock, Toot, Crack, Rock Sugar Block

- Cough and Cold Medicines - Robotripping, Robo, Tussin, Triple C, Dex, Skittles, Candy, Velvet, Lean (Purple Drank)

- Heroin - Smack, Junk, H, Black Tar, Ska, Horse

- Inhalants - Laughing Gas, Snappers, Poppers, Whippets, Texas shoeshine

- Marijuana - Pot, Grass, Herb, Weed, Mary Jane, Reefer, Skunk

- MDMA (Ecstasy or Molly) - E, XTC, X, Adam, Hug, Beans, Clarity, Love Drug, Domex (Mixed with PCP)

- Methamphetamine (Meth) - Speed, Chalk, Tina, Ice, Crystal, Crank, Glass, Go fast, Crank

- Morphine – Mary, M, Miss Emma, Mister Black, Monkey, Mojo, Mud

- Opioids – Speedball (Cocaine w/heroin)

Prescription drugs are popular with youth and are becoming the most abused substances.

- Prescription Drugs - Oxy, Percs, Vikes, Barbs, Reds, Candy, Tranks, Speed, Ritalin/Adderall (ADHD drugs)

- Prescription Depressant Medications - Barbs, Reds, Red birds, Phennies, Tooies, Yellows, Yellow jackets, Candy, Downers, Sleeping pills, Tranks,

A-minus, Zombie pills

- Prescription Stimulant Medications (Amphetamines) - Skippy, the Smart Drug, Vitamin R, Bennies, Black beauties, Roses, Hearts, Speed, Uppers

- Prescription Pain Medications (Opioids) - Hillbilly heroin, Oxy, OC, Oxycotton, Percs, Happy pills, Vikes

- Salvia - Salvia divinorum, Shepherdess's Herb, Maria Pastora, Sally-D, Ska Pastora

- Spice - K2, Fake Weed, Yucatan Fire, Skunk, Moon Rocks

- Tobacco, Nicotine & E-Cigarettes (Vaping) - Smokes, Cigs, Chew, Dip, Snuff; E-hookah, Vape sticks, Vape pens

* Many of these can be psychologically and physically addictive.

COMMONLY ABUSED DRUGS

Drug Name	Other Names	What Do They Look Like?	How Are They Used?	Negative Effects
Amphetamines	Speed, meth, crank, crystal, ice, uppers, black beauties, footballs, glass	Capsules, pills, tablets, white powder, rock resembling wax, shards of glass	Can be taken orally, injected, snorted or smoked	Irritability, anxiety, increased blood pressure, aggression convulsions, loss of appetite addiction, increased heart rate, violent behavior.
Cocaine/Crack	Coke, snow, nose candy, flake, blow, big C, lady white, snowbirds	Cocaine: white crystalline powder. Crack-salt-form, white to tan pellets or crystalline rocks that look like soap	Cocaine is inhaled or injected. Crack is smoked.	Elevated blood pressure, elevated heart rate, seizures, death by cardiac arrest or respiratory failure, depression associated w/withdrawal.
Designer Drugs	Synthetic heroin, Goodfella, Ecstasy	Tablets, capsules, powders	Injected, sniffed, smoked, or swallowed	Psychiatric disturbances, including panic, confusion anxiety, depression, paranoid thinking.
Herbal Ecstasy	Cloud 9, Rave Energy, Ultimate Xphoria, X	Pills sold in colorful packaging	Swallowed, snorted, or smoked	Seizures, heart attacks, strokes, death
Heroin	Smack, horse, mud, brown sugar, junk, black tar, big H, dope	White to dark brown powder or tar-like substance	Injected, smoked, or inhaled	Slowed and slurred speech, vomiting, "nodding off", HIV infection from injection, addiction, death from overdose.
Ice	Meth, speed, crank, crystal, batu, shabu, glass	Clear crystal chunks, like ice	Usually smoked, sometimes snorted or injected	Suppressed appetite, mood swings and unpredictable, violent behavior, coma or death, stroke

COMMONLY ABUSED DRUGS

Drug Name	Other Names	What Do They Look Like?	How Are They Used?	Negative Effects
Inhalants	Nitrous oxide, laughing gas, whip-pets, aerosol sprays, cleaning fluids, solvents	Vapors are inhaled	Nitrous oxide comes in a metal cylinder, sold in balloon or whipped cream aerosol spray can. Other inhalants include common household products like spray paint, gas, correction fluid, paint thinner and glue	Headache, muscle weakness, abdominal pain, nausea, hearing loss, limb spasms, bone marrow damage, liver & kidney damage, brain damage, coma, fatigue, lack of coordination, hepatitis, permanent damage to the nervous system, death-usually caused by a very high concentration of fumes
Marijuana/ Hashish	Weed, pot, reef-er, grass, dope, ganja, mary jane, sinsemilla, hash, herb, Aunt Mary, skunk, boom, kif, gangster, chronic	Marijuana looks like dried parsley, with stems and/or seeds which are rolled into cigarettes. Hashish looks like brown or black cakes or balls.	Usually smoked and sometimes eaten.	Increased heart rate, blood-shot eyes, reduced ability to perform tasks requiring concentration, such as driving a car, paranoia, intense anxiety or panic attacks, impairments in learning and memory, perception and judgment-difficulty speaking, listening effectively, thinking, retaining knowledge, problem solving and forming concepts.
Mushrooms	Shrooms, caps, magic mushrooms	Dried mushrooms	Eaten, brewed and drank as tea	Increased blood pressure, sweating, nausea, nervous feeling, visual changes.
PCP	Angel dust, ozone, wack, rocket fuel, peace pill, elephant, tranquilizer, dust	White crystalline powder, tablets, colored powder, liquid	Snorted, smoked, eaten, injected.	Hallucinations, "out of body" experiences, impaired motor coordination, death (more often results from accidental injury or suicide during PCP intoxication), depression, anxiety, aggressive behavior and violence.
Rohypnol	Roach, roofies, the forget pill, rope, rophies, ruffies, R2, roofe-nol, la roche, rib "Date Rape" drug	A small white tablet with no taste or odor when dissolved in a drink	Swallowed as a pill, dissolved in a drink or snorted.	Blackouts, with complete loss of memory, addiction, overdose (rare), dizziness and disorientation, nausea

COMMONLY ABUSED DRUGS

Drug Name	Other Names	What Do They Look Like?	How Are They Used?	Negative Effects
Special K	Vitamin K, K2, new Exstasy, psychedelic heroin, Ketalar, Ketaject, Super-K, breakfast cereal	White powder, similar to cocaine	Snorted or smoked.	Delirium, impaired motor function, potentially fatal respiratory problems, convulsion vomiting when mixed with alcohol, depressed person can become suicidal, agitated person can become violent.
LSD	Acid, microdot, tabs, doses, trips, hits or sugar cubes	Colored tablets, blotter paper, clear liquid and thin squares of gelatin	Taken orally, licked off paper. Gelatin and liquid can be put in the eyes	Potentially devastating psychiatric effects, elevated blood pressure, sleeplessness, tremors, chronic recurring hallucinations (flashbacks)
Steroids	Rhoids, juice	Tablets or liquid	Orally or injected into muscle.	Liver tumors, sterility, masculine traits in women, aggression, depression associated with withdrawal, jaundice, high blood pressure, severe acne, trembling.
Tobacco & E-Cigarettes	Dip, chew, fags (cigarettes), smoke, Vaping	Cigarettes, cigars, pipe tobacco, smokeless (chew, dip, snuff) E-cigs; E-hookah, Vape Sticks; Vape pens	Usually smoked. Sometimes tobacco leaves are "dipped" or "chewed" so the nicotine is absorbed via the gums.	Heart and cardiovascular disease, cancers of the lung, larynx, esophagus, bladder, pancreas, kidney & mouth, emphysema and chronic bronchitis, spontaneous abortion, preterm birth; low birth weight and fetal death when used during pregnancy.
Alcohol	Beer, wine, liquor, wine cooler, malt liquor, booze	Liquid	Drunk	Dizziness, slurred speech disturbed sleep, nausea, vomiting, hangovers, impaired motor skills, violent behavior, impaired learning, fetal alcohol syndrome, respiratory failure, depression and death (high doses) and addiction (alcoholism).

Source: Drug-Free Resource Net Partnership for a Drug-Free America

THE DANGERS OF DRUG USE

Alcohol, tobacco, vaping, and other drug use can lead to unwanted sexual activity, unwanted pregnancies, illness, death, violence, deadly driving, and other destructive behavior including:

- Death by cardiac arrest (heart attack), overdose, or drug related violence

- Increased risk of exposure to HIV/AIDS and COVID-19

- Diseases directly related to drug use including hepatitis, cancer, and HIV/AIDS

- Addiction – when your body becomes dependent on a particular substance

- Lying, stealing, and cheating to get drugs and/or money for drugs

- Depression and paranoia and other mental health problems

- Loss of trust from family and friends

- Grades suffering, dropping out of school, and destroyed dreams

- Tremors and seizures, which can result in coma or death

- Strokes

WHY DO SOME GIRLS USE DRUGS?

- Girls often experience lower self-esteem during their early teenage years

- Peer pressure, pressure to fit in, and pressure to be physically attractive and please others

- Copying behavior seen at home, in the neighborhood, in the movies, on social media, or heard in music

- To escape from reality; their lives may be very sad or difficult

- No adult has talked to them about drugs

TIPS FOR STAYING AWAY FROM DRUGS

- Ask your parents/guardians/caring adults to listen to you when you have something to say or when you are finding it hard to deal with things going on in your life – like COVID-19, relationships, or school.

- Ask your parents/guardians to role play how to say NO scenarios.

- Ask for information that is appropriate for your age. Between the ages of 12 and 17, it is a good idea to learn what certain drugs look like, their street names, and how they can affect your body.

- Have a clear position on drugs - A "JUST SAY NO" policy with research to back your decision.

- Get support in learning social skills. Young people who don't have good friends are more likely to get involved with drugs and alcohol than young people who have close relationships with their peers.

- Find ways to build self-esteem - including hanging out with positive peers.

- Develop interests that are positive. Becoming involved in healthy activities, such as a hobby, church, after-school/community activities, or some type of fitness activity keeps you busy and more likely to stay away from drugs.

- Learn how to evaluate media messages. Movies, music, magazines, social media, and television bombard young people with distorted messages about drugs and alcohol, making it seem like they're cool to use. With an adult's guidance, you can learn the real deal about what you see and hear.

- If you think you, or someone you know, might have a problem, seek help. Talk to your parents or guardians or another trusted adult. There are also some resources at the end of this chapter and books that may be helpful. USE THEM!

- These tips will help you in developing your stand against drugs and alcohol. Share them with family members and friends.

WHAT'S ON YOUR MIND?

Share your situations, questions, or concerns about drugs, tobacco, vaping, and alcohol.

....

....

Have you been approached to use drugs or try alcohol, tobacco, or vaping?

....

....

Have you ever tried illegal substances? Are you using any now?

....

....

What do you do to stay away from drugs and alcohol? How do you "Just Say NO?"

....

....

Drop me a line and tell me what YOU would say if you were one of the Angels at the beginning of this chapter. My website is in the back of the book. Can't wait to hear from you.

Resources:

https://www.drugabuse.gov/drugs-abuse

Classifications of Drugs – https://www.addictioncenter.com/drugs/drug-classifications/

https://teens.drugabuse.gov/drug-facts

https://dare.org/drug-legalization-and-student-drug-use

www.drugfree.org

TEENS AND GAMBLING

What is gambling? Any time you risk something of value (money or something else) for the chance to win, you are gambling. Gambling is a popular past time in US culture, can be addictive, and is against the law for minors.

There are many ways to gamble:

Some gambling, like lotteries, slot machines, or bingo depend on luck and no amount of knowledge or practice can help you win.

Other games like pool or darts require skills. So, knowing how to play influences the results.

Card games involve chance and some amount of skill. The skill in card games comes from knowing what to do with the hand you are dealt. The more a person knows about playing, the more it can increase the chances of winning. But a win is never guaranteed because part of the game involves chance. A player has no control over the cards being dealt. Even the best player can carry a losing hand.

Internet gambling is becoming popular. It is easy to access online venues that can quickly become a problem. A problem that will most likely affect not just the gambler, but that person's family and friends.

Many teens try out different gambling activities like bingo, poker, lottery tickets, dice, scratch cards, sports betting, and more. Approximately 60-80% of high school students report having gambled for money recently.

Most people gamble on occasion and for fun. Others gamble excessively and may develop serious problems.

4-5% of youth (ages 12-17) meet one or more criteria of having a gambling problem.

10-14% of youth (ages 12-17) are at risk of developing a gambling addiction.

Although boys are more likely than girls to gamble and experience gambling problems, the numbers of girls who gamble is on the rise.

Why Do Teens Gamble?

Teens often start gambling because someone in their family gambles or their friends are into it. Many teens say they gamble when they are bored or lonely. Teens who developed problems say they used gambling to escape or avoid problems at home.

Here are some helpful questions to ask about gambling:

- Is it good for me?

- Even if it is fun, is it worth my time?
- What are the risks?

Why Gambling is a Problem

- Excessive gambling costs money. Hot winning streaks only occur from time to time --often there is a loss.
- Gambling affects personality, causing mood swings and social life and relationship problems.
- Gambling can also affect a person's health, causing sleep problems, anxiety, stress, depression, unexplained anger, thoughts of suicide, and suicide attempts.
- People with a severe gambling addiction can gamble away everything they have. Some resort to stealing to fuel their habit. When people skip school, or miss work to gamble, there is a problem.

The Risks:

- Teens who enjoy taking risks or who have trouble controlling their impulses have a higher chance of becoming addicted to gambling. Usually, these issues will not happen automatically, but they are more likely to get sucked in.

Resources:

High School Gambling Fact Sheet - www.ncpgambling.org/files/HS_Fact_Sheet.pdf

Gambling and Teenagers -- https://raisingchildren.net.au/pre-teens/behaviour/behaviour-questions-issues/gambling

Section contributed by Dr. Glenda Clare | Family Partner Specialist, Center for Family & Community Engagement at NC State University

TEENAGE VIOLENCE IN AMERICA

Youth violence is a serious public health problem and an *Adverse Childhood Experience* (ACE) that can have long-term impact on health and wellbeing. Youth Violence is the intentional use of physical force or power to threaten or harm others by young people ages 10-24. It typically involves young people hurting peers who are unrelated to them and who they may or may not know well. Youth violence can include fighting, bullying, threats with weapons, and gang-related violence. A young person can be involved with youth violence as a victim, offender, or witness. Youth violence has serious and lasting effects on the physical, mental, and social health of young people. It is a leading cause of death for young people and results in more than 400,000 nonfatal injuries each year. The impact of youth violence goes beyond physical consequences. (April 7, 2020 | CDC 24/7: Saving Lives, Protecting People™)

My prayer is that you learn about the dangers of violence, develop self-love and self- respect, and make life-enhancing choices for yourself. Peace and serenity are two of life's best gifts; enjoy them. There are things you can do to help stop the violence and promote peace and serenity.

They include:

- Listen to adults who tell you that guns and other weapons can hurt and kill.

- Learn how to resolve conflicts without resorting to negative words or actions:

  1. To mediate a conflict, seek out adults who are setting positive examples.

  2. Treat others the way you want to be treated.

  3. Use humor to cool hostility.

  4. Follow the "No Guns/Weapons" policy at your school. Report to school authorities any knowledge about weapons (anonymously, if possible).

  5. Participate in programs that teach problem solving, assertiveness, conflict resolution, and other interpersonal skills.

  6. Don't be a victim. Learn safety rules, how to say NO and mean it, and how to scream and make lots of noise if a stranger tries to touch you or take you away.

  (Source: Modified from Teen Violence Homepage Website)

DATE RAPE & SEXUAL ASSAULT

The definition of date rape is having sex, against your will with someone you are dating.

Some girls think this is acceptable behavior from their friend or partner. It is unacceptable behavior. DO NOT ACCEPT THIS BEHAVIOR FROM ANYONE!

Many young girls get into relationships too early and/or with partners who are not healthy. Unhealthy relationships can become violent and sometimes deadly. Before you get into a relationship with anyone, take time to get to know yourself, learn what is important to you, and develop standards of excellence and a bottom line!

How to avoid date rape or assault:

1. Make a commitment to yourself to have sex when you are ready. Make that clear to the individual(s) you date.

2. When you do start dating, hang out with other couples or with groups who engage in positive activities. Limit your time alone together. Never go places where you are uncomfortable.

3. At parties or other outings, never leave your drink unattended. If you do, don't drink from it when you return. Individuals can slip in drugs that will make you sluggish or unconscious, making it easier for them to take advantage of you.

4. Stop hanging out with negative people, and particularly disrespectful individuals. It's not cute to be called a "b--" or a "h-."

What to do if you are raped or sexually assaulted:

Being raped or sexually assaulted can be scary, confusing, and traumatic, but healing is possible. Know that what you might be feeling is a normal reaction to trauma and there is hope. TRIGGER WARNING: Some of this information may be a trigger for some rape survivors.

Things to do to get started on the road to healing

1. Go someplace safe, like a friend's home or the hospital.
   - *If you still feel unsafe – call 911 or the National Sexual Assault Hotline (800-656-4673).*

2. Leave your body as is. Even though you might be anxious to take a shower, it is important to leave all the evidence as is.

3. Don't even brush your teeth, comb your hair, eat, smoke, or take any medication.

4. Get medical treatment. It is understandable that you don't want anyone else to touch you right now, but you need to get a medical examination right away.

5. Decide if you want to talk to the police. Even though what has happened to you is a crime, it is 100% your decision whether you press charges or not.

THE ROAD TO RECOVERY:

a. As a survivor, you may experience depression, thoughts of suicide, flashbacks, and PTSD (Post Traumatic Stress Disorder). Others may experience self-destructive behaviors, such as self-harming, eating disorders, or substance abuse as ways to cope. But these do not have to be your reality.

b. Find healthy ways to cope through outside therapy, support groups, recovery programs, and supportive friends and family.

GIRLS AND GANGS

Many communities and some schools have serious gang problems. All gangs spell trouble. They cause fear, destroy property, hurt people, and destroy businesses and schools. Street gangs aren't made up of just boys anymore. Today, they are made up of girls and are just as dangerous as the traditional gangs you hear and know about. Girl gangs are on the rise, along with the number of girls joining them. Hopefully, the adults in your life have made it very clear that they will not tolerate your involvement in a gang, and you do not find it necessary or desirable to join one.

Why Some Girls Join Gangs:

- To belong to a group.

- To have a place of acceptance.

- To gain respect and power.

- For excitement – to get attention, attend parties, and do drugs.

- For protection if they are being picked on by other gangs.

- To earn money to help at home or buy nice clothes, etc.

- Peer pressure - they have been threatened.

- It's a way of life in their neighborhood or school.

- Lack of support network - real or imagined problems at home that make them prefer the streets.

- Racism and poverty - when groups of people are denied access to power, privileges, and resources, they form their own anti-establishment groups.

- Media influences - television, movies, radio, and music that promote gang life as an acceptable lifestyle.

Dangers of Gangs:

- Girl gangs usually require new members to be initiated with activities that can be violent and dangerous - including stealing, fighting, sexual acts, and even murder.

- Girl gang members often become involved in illegal activities such as selling and using drugs, violence, using weapons, and more.

- Girl gangs are making their way into schools and bringing danger with them.

- Girls in gangs are at risk of injury or death because of their involvement - fights, retaliation for crimes committed, or just being targeted for being a member of a certain gang.

- Girls could also get kicked out of school or go to jail for crimes they commit or get swept up with a gang that has done something wrong.

TIPS FOR STAYING OUT OF GANGS:

- Pray to God for strength and safety.

  - Become active in a positive community or church group.

- Learn to love and respect yourself - find value in your own life.

- Try to establish a positive connection at home or with a trusted adult in your neighborhood or at school.

- Stay in school. Make education your priority.

- Learn conflict resolution skills.

  - Join peer-counseling or other support groups.

- Participate in positive activities: sports, music, drama, and other community activities.

- These activities help build a sense of self-worth and self-respect.

  - Take a self-defense class.

- Hang around with positive girls.

- Ask to move to a different neighborhood. If you are unable to move, ask a caring relative if they would be willing to let you stay with them.

LET'S GET REAL

1. Have you ever been the victim of violence?

   ....

2. Have you been violent toward others?

   ....

3. Do you or someone you know belong to a gang?

   ....

4. Do you feel safe in your home, neighborhood, or school? If not, why not?

   ....

5. Do you carry a weapon or know someone who does?

   ....

6. What would you do if you were threatened?

   ....

7. Do you need help right now?

   ....

Refer to the HOTLINE page if you need help NOW!

Violence is everywhere. However, there is hope for you and your generation. You were placed on this earth to be happy, joyful, and free. Use information in this guide and call on your GIGO Guardian Angels to guide you through your life.

Waiting Until Adulthood/Marriage to Have Sex
Abstinence: It's the Smart Choice

What do you know about sex, anyway? Adolescents learn about sex:

- From their friends

- From school

- From the media

- From their parents or guardians or other adults

Sexual intimacy, when the time is right, can be a very pleasurable experience. Allow yourself time to be a child, a teenager, and blossom into womanhood without the pressures and consequences that can come from early sexual activity. The gift of your body and soul, through the act of making love should be shared with a loving, committed partner only when you are old enough, mature enough, and responsible enough to appreciate it.

Look forward to making love not just having sex.

Many young people have too much information and others don't know anything.

GET THE FACTS STRAIGHT!

WHAT IS SEXUAL INTERCOURSE?

Sexual intercourse is intimate physical contact between two people: male to female, female to female and/or male to male. Intimate physical contact may include fingering or going into a body part such as the vagina (vaginal sex), the anus/butt (anal sex), or the mouth (oral sex).

If a young girl has sex, it can result in:

- Pregnancy (sex with a boy) - if the male sperm (present in the fluid that comes from the male penis during sex) is successful in fertilizing a ripened female egg. Yes, you can get pregnant the FIRST time you have sex.

- Sexually transmitted diseases, including HIV/AIDS. There is more information about them at the end of the chapter.

- Loss of self-respect.

- A reputation as a⎯⎯⎯⎯ , or⎯⎯⎯⎯ , or⎯⎯⎯⎯ (you fill in the blanks).

Sexual intercourse has many other common names. List some of the ones you have heard:

1. ....

2. ....

3. ....

4. ....

5. ....

Sexual activity includes more than just the act of sexual intercourse. It also includes anal penetration, oral sex, and mutual masturbation. Ask a trusted and respectful adult (not your friends) to define these terms if you are not familiar with them. Being a virgin means not doing ANY of these things. Many teens think these activities are acceptable because they aren't having sex. They are WRONG! These activities can also lead to deadly consequences and lower self-esteem.

CONSEQUENCES OF EARLY SEXUAL ACTIVITY

Young people who are not married or in an adult committed relationship, and engage in sexual activity are more likely to face the following problems:

- A greater number of sexual partners and increased risk for Sexually

Transmitted Diseases (STDs) or AIDS.

- Lack of respect for themselves and their partner(s).
- Lack of honesty with partner(s) like not being truthful about having an STD or AIDS.

These problems are more likely to happen the younger you become sexually active.

Why not remain a virgin until adulthood/marriage and skip all the pain and stress? Don't let the media or other young people try to convince you that you must have sex to be accepted or to enjoy life. Over 50% of teens are not "DOING IT." They are abstaining from sex, which is the best and ONLY 100% effective way to avoid pregnancy or STDs.

What Happens When Things Don't Work Out?

Girls, more so than boys, attach deep feelings to a sexual experience. If things don't work out, or when the relationship ends, especially if you are not in a committed adult relationship or married it can lead to:

- Disappointment
- Pain
- Embarrassment
- A bad reputation
- Depression

Don't think that girls are the only ones trying to wait until marriage or a committed adult relationship. I know a 15-year-old boy who told his girlfriend he wouldn't have sex because he wanted his wife to be his first. They developed a comfortable, closer relationship without worrying about whether to have sex. If a partner cares about you, they will respect your wishes and not pressure you.

If they try to make you feel bad because you want to wait, *KICK THEM TO THE CURB!*

Sex was not intended to be shameful, dirty, or at-risk behavior. Learn to wait and appreciate it for the special experience it is meant to be. Unfortunately, there are some girls who have chosen (or have been forced - that's what rape means) to engage in sexual activity before they are ready.

DID YOU KNOW?

More than 4 out of 10 young women become pregnant before they reach the age of 20 - nearly one million a year.

- More than 8 out of 10 of these pregnancies are unplanned.

- Almost 75 percent of births to teens are outside of marriage, up from only 15 percent 30 years ago.

- One of every 3 girls has had sexual intercourse by the age of 16, and 1 out of 2 by the age of 18.

- Teen mothers are less likely to complete high school and more likely to end up on welfare.

- 22,000 babies are abandoned each year in hospitals and in the streets - many were births to teens feeling they had nowhere else to turn.

You can lower these statistics by not being among these numbers.

(Source: The National Campaign to Prevent Teen Pregnancy)

Sexually Transmitted Diseases (STDs)

Sex is not dangerous or gross. It can be a wonderful, worry-free experience. However, it's best when you are a mature, informed, and consenting adult. As an adolescent girl, you need to know the dangers of STD's because they can also occur when you are an adult. This is another reason to postpone sexual activity until you are in an adult relationship with someone you know and trust.

- STDs are sometimes called venereal diseases.

- They are common, avoidable, but not all are curable.

- Each year 1 out of 4 sexually active females between fifteen and nineteen seek treatment for a STD.

- You can have a STD without knowing it.

- Some STDs can give you cancer. Others can make you sterile (not able to have a baby) or drive you insane.

- You CAN'T get STDs from toilet seats, hot tubs, swimming pools, or bugs.

- You CAN get STDs from unprotected vaginal, anal, or oral sex with an infected partner.

HIV, which is a virus, is transmitted through bodily fluids. It can be contracted by:

- Sexual activity.

- Blood transfusions.

- Sharing infected needles through drug use.

- Being stuck with an infected needle through tattooing, body piercing, or in a health care setting - for example, getting punctured in the hospital with an infected needle.

- During pregnancy, birth, or breast-feeding, an infected mother can pass it on to her baby.

This section will describe several of the most common STDs. Refer to additional sources for more information.

Chlamydia

This is the most common STD. Most infected females have no symptoms until there are complications. The highest infection rate of any group seems to be girls fifteen to nineteen. Antibiotics can cure Chlamydia, but it must be detected and treated. It can cause infertility if it goes untreated.

HPV or Genital Warts

The Human Papillomavirus (HPV) is highly contagious. The warts, which appear on the genitals and are sometimes hard to see, can be removed but may come back. Some kinds are non-cancerous. Others are known to cause cervical cancer. There is no known cure for HPV.

Gonorrhea

Also known as the "clap," a female has a 50% chance of getting Gonorrhea from an infected partner. It is curable, but if left untreated, it can lead to arthritis, heart trouble, or pelvic inflammatory disease (PID), which, can scar the fallopian tubes, making it hard or impossible to have a baby.

Trichomoniasis

Trichomoniasis is hard to detect and extremely common but treatable. It is very irritating, and symptoms won't go away without treatment.

Genital Herpes

Incurable, this highly contagious virus is spread by direct contact. It is a lifetime recurring disease that can cause brain damage and death in infants. It can appear as cold sores or blisters in the mouth, genital or rectal area, or thighs. Condoms don't always protect against herpes because sores can be in places condoms can't cover.

Hepatitis B

Treatable, this virus that attacks the liver is spread through sexual contact or contaminated needles. Hepatitis B is carried in blood, semen, saliva, and urine.

Hepatitis C

Also treatable but hard to detect, this virus attacks the liver too. It is spread through unclean needles and from sex with a carrier.

Syphilis

Early syphilis can be cured, sometimes with a single shot of penicillin. Without treatment, syphilis can severely damage your heart, brain, or other organs and can be life-threatening. Syphilis can also be passed from mothers to unborn children.

HIV/AIDS

A disease for which there is no known cure that has devastated millions around the world. There is treatment, though, and with proper medical care the disease can be controlled. AIDS weakens the body's immune system and makes it unable to ward off certain infections, pneumonias, and cancers.

The HIV virus is spread through blood and bodily fluids. It is also spread through sexual activity with an infected partner (vaginal, anal, and oral sex), sharing dirty drug needles or being stuck accidentally in a health care setting, blood transfusions, and by an infected pregnant woman to her baby. Anyone can get AIDS.

(Source: Center for Disease Control & National Institute of Allergy and Infectious Diseases)

It is very important to know about these diseases. Use this information to begin a discussion with a trusted adult. You need accurate guidance from someone who has experience with these issues.

Your future is in your hands. Now that you have this information, you do not need to experience it first-hand. Make decisions that will enable you to lead a happy, healthy, and whole life free of any of these diseases and the bad feelings they bring.

A PAGE FOR YOUR POSITIVE THOUGHTS
(END OF CHAPTER CHECK-IN!)

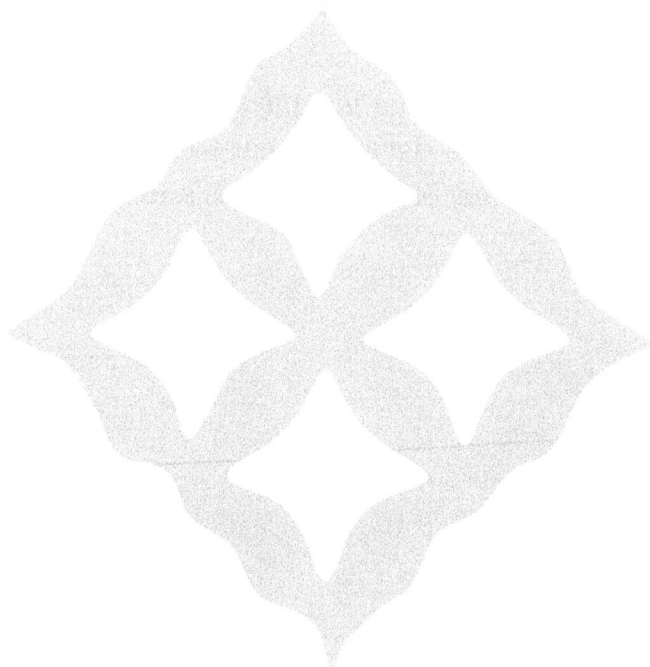

CONVERSATIONS WITH
JOY, FAITH, LOVE, AND GRACE

Let's empower all girls to find their positive place in the world, help others when we can, and help raise money so others can live better lives.

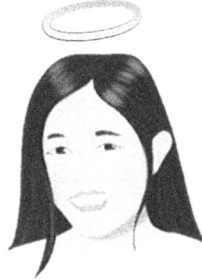

I might not be able to hear, but sure can smell. It makes me sad when girls don't have good hygiene and they stink. I'm going to share this handbook with them.

My personal style is simple yet stylish. Thats why I believe BALD IS BEAUTIFUL! I am honoring my battle with cancer and all those who are touched with this crappy disease.

I like the way I look without makeup, but I am learning how to enhance my eyes, cheeks, and lips without looking like a clown.

"WE'VE GOT IT GOIN' ON! WE FEEL GOOD ON THE INSIDE. WE LOOK GOOD ON THE OUTSIDE. WITH A LITTLE FAITH, A LITTLE HOPE, AND A LOT OF LOVE, WE ARE GOING TO MAKE A DIFFERENCE IN THIS WORLD!"

Standard of Excellence #9

Looking Your Best
Grooming, Hair Care, and Fashion

(Symbol of good feminine qualities: patience, fondness, love and care)

YOUR PERSONAL STYLE

Personal style begins with what you see in the mirror. Repeat after me:

MIRROR, MIRROR
ON THE WALL

WHO'S THE GREATEST OF
THEM ALL?

MY, OH MY,
IT MUST BE ME –

BECAUSE I'M THE ONLY
ONE I SEE!

You create YOUR own style. Developing good grooming habits – loving and caring for your hair and skin and choosing affordable clothes that are right for you – that's style!

When your inner-light shines and you have self-love, you will learn how much your appearance says about you. You are a unique creation. Your style should reflect you . . . saying something only you can say. And say it with self-respect.

There are lots of great clothes and hairstyles appropriate for your age. So many girls and young women (older women too) wear tight pants or skirts, skirts that are too short, and tops that show too much of their breasts. The media also encourages girls to look and act older than they are. This promotes inappropriate, suggestive dressing. You will not get a partner, or live a better life, simply by dressing like the females in the ads or on television, or social media.

Don't believe the hype! Make your choices based on self-awareness and self-respect.

Personal style begins with the basics – good grooming. Grooming is the external care that tends to focus on improving your outer appearance. Develop good grooming habits early in life, so they will stick with you.

"I think self-confidence comes from you and your heart. You don't need anybody to tell you that you look good. You need to know that for a fact. That's one thing I think Sistahs need to improve in their character."

Ayisha Wells (14-years old | Washington, DC)

GOOD GROOMING HABITS

Cleaning Your Face: It is important to clean your face at least twice a day, using a face wash and a moisturizer, instead of soap.

Cleaning Your Nose: It is important to clean your nose every day. Let someone know (without telling the whole world - maybe pull them aside) if they have something in their nose or anywhere on their face - remember, unless you look in the mirror, you won't see it. I'm sure YOU would appreciate it.

Cleaning Your Eyes: Use a clean, damp washcloth to clean the area around your eyes daily.

Cleaning Your Ears: Put a clean, damp washcloth over your index finder and wash in and around each ear. As an old saying goes, "Never put anything smaller than your elbow in your ear."

Cleaning Your Mouth: It is important to brush your teeth at least twice a day and floss them twice a day. Also, change your toothbrush every three months. Remember to get regular dental check-ups. Use mouthwash to help prevent cavities and strengthen teeth.

Cleaning Your Body: It is important to take a shower or bath every day. If you usually shower, you may want to take a bath once a week to loosen ground-in dirt. This is important so you don't start smelling.

Protecting Your Skin: After your shower or bath, lotion your body. Lotion helps replace the moisture that is lost from bathing, excessive sunlight, and polluted air. Be sure to put extra lotion on your hands, elbows, knees, and heels.

Feminine Hygiene: Keep your vaginal area clean. During your menstrual cycle, bathe, or shower regularly, change your feminine products, and be aware of any odors which is your signal to bathe again or change your tampons or pads.

Smelling Good: Use underarm deodorant after a shower, bath, or wash-up.

For an extra special smell, you may want to use a body spray, but don't overdo it. You may also use bath gel, lotions, or powders.

Caring for Your Feet and Hands: Keep your fingernails neat, clean, manicured (learn how to do them yourself - it will save you a bundle that you could otherwise be investing) and at a reasonable length - claws are creepy. Designs are nice, but don't get carried away. Choose colors that are flattering on you.

Keep your feet clean and well-manicured. That means cut those toenails. Nail polish can be nice, especially in the summer when you wear sandals. Always get permission from your parent or guardian as to whether you can start wearing polish. Lotion your hands and feet. It keeps them soft and beautiful.

I have smelled girls while walking down the street or in a school hallway. It is not pleasant. The odors include body odor, menstrual odor, bad breath, musty armpits, and dirty clothes.

This is not funny or cute.

Take pride in yourself. Keep yourself and your clothes clean and neat. Be a friend and help someone who seems to be having a problem or find an adult and ask them to speak to her. You never know what their circumstances may be.

Style That Hair!!!

There are wonderful differences in girls' hair length, color, and texture.

Learn about your hair type and what you need to do to make the most of what you were born/blessed with. Hair length, color, and texture should be a source of pride and joy. Self-esteem can be affected by the way you feel about your hair. There is no such thing as "good" or "bad" hair – ALL hair is the Creator's gift. Learn to love what's on top of your head, whether it is long, medium, short, coarse, wavy, kinky, nappy, or straight. If you are unable to achieve a certain look without a major overhaul, it's not for you. Find another style that you really like that you can easily create naturally.

Hair Care Basics for Teens:

1. Regularly wash and condition with shampoo that is right for your hair.

2. Get a good cut – one that fits your face, age, and lifestyle.

3. Have your hair trimmed regularly.

4. Learn the proper use for combs, brushes, blow dryers, hair accessories, etc.

5. Establish a healthy diet, rich in nutrients found in fish, beans, poultry, fruit, vegetables, and Vitamin B complex.

6. Develop a positive attitude about your hair.

Your hair is your crowning glory. Celebrate it by taking good care of it. Adding hair (weaves, braids, wigs, extensions, etc.) should only be to enhance your look, not to replace or cover up your natural hair because you are embarrassed or think your natural hair is not acceptable. Don't get caught up in social media and other platforms that overemphasize the length and texture of the women being featured. Also, don't worry about what the boys say.

What do you do to get ready for school?

Write your routine below:

1. Pick out my clothes the night before (cleaned and pressed).

2. Floss and brush my teeth.

3. Wash my face and ears.

4. Take a shower/bath.

5. Make my lunch or be sure to have payment for lunch.

6. Gather my books.

7. ....

8. ....

9. ....

10. ....

11. ....

12. ....

13. ....

14. ....

15. ....

WHAT ABOUT MAKE-UP?

Make-up is used to enhance, NOT HIDE, your natural beauty. You want to create a look that is appealing and natural, not a Halloween mask. According to Tyra Banks' book, *Tyra's BEAUTY – Inside & Out*, "The key to any make-up routine is keep it real." Make-up can enhance your natural facial attributes: eyes, cheekbones, or mouth. Keep in mind that less is more. You can create different looks for different occasions – school, church, or a party.

Every girl does not have to wear make-up. It is a personal choice (first, get permission).

Don't let other girls pressure you into doing something you are not ready for or comfortable with.

Fashion Tips for Teens

Pulling it all together! Almost every girl wants to be in style. Your clothes say a lot about you. It is not only what you wear, but how you wear it. Make sure your clothes are appropriate and send the right message. Remember, what's right for you may not be right for someone else and vice versa. Consider your height, weight, other physical features, and the event or occasion. The media (TikTok, Instagram, television, etc.) exposes girls to many inappropriate ways of dressing.

Experiment by finding colors and shapes that work for you (clothes, hair, and make-up):

- First, make sure that your clothes are neat, clean, and pressed, and express your personality.

- Find YOUR LOOK by trying on lots of clothes and different styles. You can do it now using different online programs without even having to be in the store.

- Volunteer to model for a store, community organization, or church fashion show.

- For suggestions, ask an older sister, cousin, friend, your mom, or another adult role model. Make sure they have some style!

- Play around with hair, make-up, and accessories keeping in mind the unique style you are trying to create.

Dressing for Success

SO, WHAT'S UP WITH THAT OUTFIT??!!
Are you trying to be FIERCE? Well, you can be, by using good judgment about your fashion choices. What would you put on the lists below?

Do's	Don'ts
1. Wear clothes that are comfortable.	1. Wear clothes that are too revealing.
2.	2.
3.	3.
4.	4.

WHAT SHOULD I WEAR?

School: Check with your local malls, current issues of youth magazines, and online for what's in style and appropriate. Also, use good judgment when looking through the magazines or online. Some have girls inappropriately dressed. You do not want to imitate them. If you wear a uniform, add some style to your outfit by accessorizing. Remember not to break the school dress code. If you are on video because of homeschooling, make sure you are dressed from head to toe just in case you get up from your computer.

Place of Worship: Be respectful with your outfits. Wear dresses and skirts that have decent hemlines and necklines (ask a trusted adult if you aren't sure), pants that aren't tight or ride low on the hips, and tops that are appropriate for a place of worship even if you meet separately with the youth ministry.

The Mall or Just Hangin' Out: Same as suggested for school – be comfortable and tasteful. Some girls can't wait to get away from the glaring eyes of adults and use outings to totally change the way they dress. Sometimes you will see scantily clad or under-clothed girls in public, thinking they are cute or cool. They don't realize the danger they are putting themselves in. Be mindful that there are people you don't see looking at you and just waiting to lure you away and do you harm. Human trafficking – make sure you learn about this important topic.

A Job Interview or in the Workplace: Dress like you mean business! No matter what the position, you want your potential employer to take you seriously. Some girls dress too sloppy, too casual, or too revealing. Remember, you want a job, not a date or a part in an adult movie!

Other Occasions: Imagine that the FASHION POLICE are standing outside your door each time you leave – would you be arrested?!

DRESSING IN STYLE ON A BUDGET

How DO you do that?

Where to get your clothes:

- Online shopping
- Department stores
- Designer discount stores
- Designing and making your own clothes
- Second-hand or consignment shops
- Flea markets
- Outlet malls

Department store clearance centers

Can you think of other sources?

When you cannot afford all you want or anything you want for that matter:

1. Be grateful for what you have. Learn to want what you have so that someday you can have what you want.

2. Get back in touch with self-esteem:

   a. You are loveable even if you cannot afford all the latest stuff. You cannot control other people's actions, such as making fun of you or teasing you, but you can fight back by believing in yourself even though sometimes it can be challenging.

   b. You are worthwhile.

   c. The better you feel about yourself, the less needy you will be.

3. Be creative:

   a. Learn to design and make your own clothes.

   b. Learn to bargain hunt. Yes, you can find great style for a lot less.

   c. Get a job.

You do not have to spend a lot of money to look like a million bucks, especially with so many resources in your community and online. Have fun with your personal fashion statement. Being the best that you can be begins and ends with you. Remember, feeling your best on the inside will help you look and feel your best on the outside. And always remember these words if other people start talking about you – PEOPLE WHO JUDGE DON'T MATTER . . . AND PEOPLE WHO MATTER DON'T JUDGE!

BE YOURSELF! HONOR YOURSELF! LOVE YOURSELF!

A PAGE FOR YOUR POSITIVE THOUGHTS
(END OF CHAPTER CHECK-IN!)

CONVERSATIONS WITH GRACE, JOY, FAITH, LOVE, HOPE, PEACE, AND CHARITY

ALL GIRLS MATTER!

GRACE
LATINA

JOY
ASIAN/PACIFIC ISLANDER

FAITH
MULTI-RACIAL

LOVE
AFRICAN DESCENT

HOPE
AFRICAN DESCENT

PEACE
NATIVE AMERICAN/ALASKAN NATIVE

CHARITY
EUROPEAN DESCENT

We want to learn from our elders, but we also want them to listen to us. We look forward to gaining knowledge and wisdom from the adults in our lives – even from their mistakes.

Teach us well so that we can become the
NEXT GENERATION OF WOMEN WARRIORS!

Standard of Excellence #10

Words Of Wisdom

What Girls Really Need from the Adults In Their Lives &
A Few Words from the Adults Who Care For and About Girls

(Symbol of improvement, advancement, growth, the need for friendliness and interdependence. The development of a young person into a contributing social being is a noteworthy achievement for the family, the clan, and the nation.)

The Four "T's"

Teach Me!

Tell Me the Truth About Life!

Spend Quality Time with Me!

Demonstrate Positive Touch!

It's Our Turn to Talk!

(From Us Girls)

We might not always say it or show it, but we really do appreciate all you adults do for us and have shared with us in this handbook and hope that girls all around the world will read, learn, be empowered, and maybe tell another girl about **GOT IT GOIN' ON-II.** However, we want to end this amazing personal development and social-emotional learning resource by telling adults a few things that we think you need to know that will help you more effectively raise us, mentor us, counsel us, teach us, and LOVE US!

1. When we come home – give us a chance to unwind before you start asking us about our day or for us to do something. Give us a few minutes to breathe, but be aware and ready to be a listening, non-judgmental ear when we are ready to talk. Our lives are jam packed from the time we wake up until the time we can finally sleep and just keeping up is a daily struggle for some of us.

2. It would also be nice to regularly hear from the adults who care for and about us:

    a. "I love you."

    b. "I see you."

    c. "I hear you."

    d. "You matter."

    e. "You are valued."

    f. "You are ENOUGH and special just the way you are."

3. Stop judging us and making us feel bad and wrong. Understand that we are going to make mistakes just like you did when you were our age. This handbook will help us avoid some stuff, but the rest we are going to have to experience on

our own. Tell us it is okay to fail and allow us the space to fail. Encourage us to *fail forward* and help us celebrate and learn from our failures.

4. Be more involved and engaged in our lives, even when we push you away. It is one of the best ways to help protect us from those who might not have our best interest at heart. Most of us are not aware that our parents or guardians and other trusted adults in our lives are the most influential people in our lives right now. We think it is our friends. Do NOT give up on us - be patient. PLEASE, get us help if you cannot handle us. Check out some of the resources at the end of the handbook.

    • Get to know our friends. If we will not let you - that's a RED FLAG!
    • Get to know the parents or guardians of our friends as well.
    • Get into our heads by consistently showing an interest in what we are doing.
    • Talk with us, not at us or about us.

5. Make more culturally appropriate empowerment activities, programs, and resources, like *Got It Goin' On®*, available for us to participate in and have access to, so we will know WE ARE ENOUGH–no matter what culture we come from. This will help us develop more confidence and cultural pride.

6. Tell us we are going to GROW UP GREAT and mean it!

7. Tell us not to let anyone else define us. Give us some latitude to find our way and to navigate our way to find our purpose. Help us to become comfortable in our own skin.

8. Be a POWER OF EXAMPLE, not a bad example. Provide us with MANY different positive role models, both male and female -- people from our same backgrounds and people who do not look like us. People who are popular and people from the community we can relate to. This will also help us develop confidence in who we are, where we come from, and cultural pride.

    • Share your personal experiences with us so that we can learn. They just might help us to survive.

9. Raise us to be BOLD! Stop being a "helicopter" or "snowplow" parent always hovering, trying to control everything, and overbearing, but more of a "launcher" parent. Prepare us for life - stop trying to do everything for us. That only sets us up

for failure. Too much control can be perceived as a VOTE OF NO CONFIDENCE in us. Teach us at a young age to develop problem solving skills so we can learn how to navigate our way to womanhood.

10. LOVE & RESPECT US for who we are or become- even if you do not agree with or understand it. Talk to us, and seek support to better understand our choices so that we can keep the lines of communication open.

Here's a spot where you can add to the list:

1. Instill in us that "no" is a complete sentence!

2. ....

3. ....

4. ....

5. ....

One Last Thing . . .
(From the Adults Who Care For/About You)

WE, as adults might not always say it or show it either (sometimes because we just do not know how), but we really do want the best for you, whether we are a parent or guardian, educator, service provider, or mentor. We hope this handbook will be read by girls around the world and that you will learn something that will help you navigate your road to womanhood – that you will be empowered and inspired and maybe will tell another girl about **GOT IT GOIN' ON-II**. However, we want to end this amazing personal development and social-emotional learning resource by telling girls a few things that we think you need to know that will help you become more caring, confident, culturally, financially, mentally, socially, and spiritually competent young ladies!

Ask the adults in your life to share these **Four "Ts"** with you.

The Four "Ts":

1. Teach Me! Expect and insist (in a respectful way) that, as adults, we teach you about RIGHT & WRONG, how to solve problems, and how to get along with others. Also, make sure we teach you about respecting yourselves as females and the importance of respecting others. We need to teach you to have the confidence to speak up for yourselves and become your own best advocates. Lastly, we must teach you to understand the importance of cultural pride, a good education, and good mental, emotional, financial and physical health.

2. Tell Me the Truth About Life! We need to stop trying to shield you from the realities of life. We should find ways to share our own experiences of both failure and success with you so you will learn that you can make mistakes and survive and that you can accomplish great things and remain humble and approachable. We need to talk about the tough topics like racism, discrimination, prejudice, sexism, hate, death, poverty, abuse, violence, etc., in ways that girls will understand and get support if you do not feel comfortable.

3. Spend Quality Time with Me! Only safe and trusted adults who genuinely love and respect girls need to be spending time with them and that goes for men or women. We need to do our best to engage in authentic ways and commit time when we know we can fully focus our attention on you. We know you can spot a fake in a minute, and you can tell when adults do not want to be around. Even parents need to be aware of their time commitment.

4. Demonstrate Positive Touch! Adults must demonstrate positive touch from the day you are born and for life – such as a warm hug, a tender touch, arm around the shoulder, or an appropriately placed kiss on the forehead or cheek to let you know we care. We MUST teach you about good and bad touch so you know how to tell the difference and learn what to do when you experience a bad touch. Make sure to tell a trusted adult about other adults or peers who are being disrespectful or inappropriate – saying things or behaving in ways that are inappropriate or demanding that you engage in behavior you are not comfortable with and/or know is wrong. It might be a family member, teacher, coach, faith-based staff member (Priest, Rabbi, Pastor, or Youth Minister), community-based program personnel, or juvenile justice or law enforcement employee. Be courageous and tell – even if they tell you not to.

Ask trusted adults to add to the list:

1. ....

2. ....

3. ....

4. ....

5. ....

Share this information with other girls in your life. We want you to succeed and GROW UP GREAT! Let us know how you are doing in your life and what we can do to help make it better. You can reach us at *www.authorjaniceferebee.com*.

NOW GO OUT THERE AND CHANGE THE WORLD!

I WISH FOR YOU . . .

Comfort on difficult days,

Smiles when sadness intrudes,

Rainbows to follow the clouds,

Laughter to kiss your lips,

Sunsets to warm your heart,

Gentle hugs when spirits sag,

Friendships to brighten your being,

Beauty for your eyes to see,

Confidence for when you doubt,

Faith so that you can believe,

Courage to know yourself,

Patience to accept the truth,

And LOVE to complete your life."

You are Special, Unique, and Priceless – ONE OF A KIND!!

A PAGE FOR YOUR POSITIVE THOUGHTS
(END OF CHAPTER CHECK-IN!)

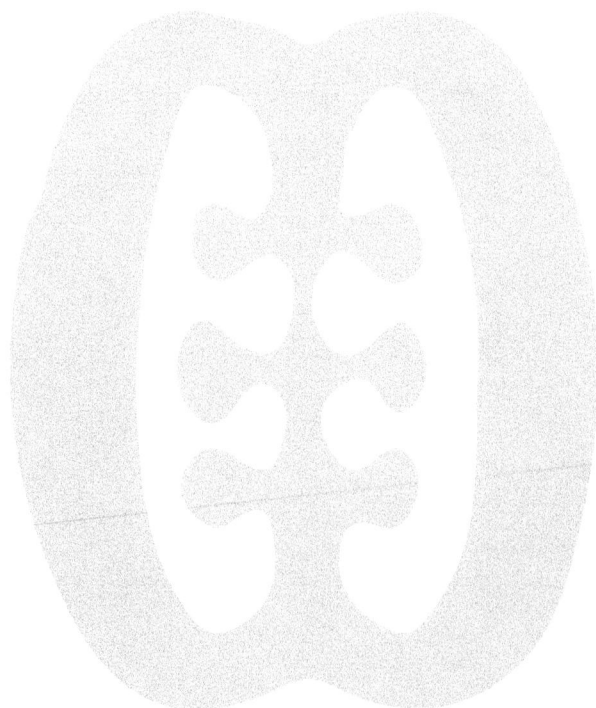

HOTLINES!
Use Them!

AIDS - National Aids Hotline	(www.cdc.gov/cdc-info	1-800-CDC-INFO (232-4636)
Alcoholics Anonymous	(The General Service Office in N.Y. - www.aa.org)	1-212-870-3400
Al-Anon (Al-Ateen) Family Group, Inc.	(www.al-anon.org)	1-888-425-2666
National Association Of Anorexia Nervosa & Associated Disorders	(www.anad.org; www.bulimia.com/topics/food-addiction-hotline/)	1-630-577-1330
Child Abuse - National Child Abuse Hotline - 24 Hour Crisis Counseling For Child Abuse And Neglect	(www.childhelp.org/childhelp-hotline/)	1-800-422-4453
Crime Victims Assistance Program	Call for Local Community Hotline	
Lesbian, Gay, Bisexual & Trans (LGBT) National Hotline	(www.glbthotline.org)	1-888-843-4564
Narcotics Anonymous -- SAMHSA'S National Hotline	(Mental & Substance Use Disorders: www.samhsa.gov/find-help/national-helpline)	1-800-662-HELP (4357)
Overeaters Anonymous N/A	www.oa.org	
Teen Pregnancy Hotline	www.americanpregnancy.org www.childwelfare.gov/topics/preventing/promoting/parenting/pregnant-teens/	1-800-672-2296
Rape, Abuse, And Incest - National Network	(www.rainn.org)	1-800-656-4673
Runaway - National Runaway Safeline	(www.800RUNAWAY.org)	1-800-RUN-AWAY (786-2929)
Suicide/Depression Crisis Lifeline	1-888-273-8255 OR call/text 988	
Teen Health & Wellness	A Variety of Hotlines/Resources www.childwelfare.gov/topics/preventing/promoting/parenting/pregnant-teens/	

EDUCATIONAL RESOURCES
(Financial Aid)

1. FINAID: The Go-to Guide for College Financial Aid (www.finaid.org)

2. The National College Resources Foundation (www.nationalcollegesresources.org)

3. Parent or Guardian's Employer

4. Financial Aid for Minority Students

5. (www.onlineschools.org; www.onlineschools.org/financial-aid/minority/)

6. Grants for Minority Students (www.collegescholarships.org/grants/minority.htm)

7. Best Colleges: Scholarships for African American & Black Students (www.bestcolleges.com/financial-aid/african-american-scholarships/)

8. www.fastweb.com

9. www.freschinfo.com

10. www.collegenet.com

11. www.embark.com

12. www.srnexpress.com

13. www.gocollege.com

14. U.S. Department of Education (www.ed.gov)

15. Financial Student Aid (www.fafsa.ed.gov)

16. College Board (www.collegeboard.org)

17. The Gates Scholarship (www.thegatesscholarship/scholarship)

18. The Gates Millennium Scholars (www.gmsp.org)

19. The United Negro College Fund (www.uncf.org)

SUGGESTED READING LIST

Recent Books:

1. Bond, Beverly: Black Girls Rock!: Owning Our Magic. Rocking Our Truth.
   (Simon & Schuster, 2018).

2. Dias, Marley: Marley Dias Gets It Done: And So Can You!
   (Scholastic, 2018).

3. Fievre, M.J. Badass Black Girl.
   (Mango Publishing, 2020).

4. Hemmen, Lucie, PhD. The Teen Girl's Survival Guide: Ten Tips for Making Friends,
   Avoiding Drama, and Coping with Social Stress
   (The Instant Help Solutions Series - Instant Help Publications, 2015)

5. Jones, Monique, L. The Book of Awesome Black Americans: Scientific Pioneers,
   Trailblazing Entrepreneurs, Barrier-Breaking Activists, and Afro-Futurists (African
   American Biographies).
   (Mango Publishers, 2020).

6. Lockington, Mariama, J. For Black Girls Like Me.
   (Macmillan Publishers, 2019).

7. Morrison, Julee. The How-To Cookbook for Teens.
   (Callisto Media, 2020).

8. Obama, Michelle. BECOMING
   (Crown Publishing, 2018).

9. Tough, Paul. How Children Succeed: Grit, Curiosity, and the Hidden Power of
   Character. (Houghton, Mifflin, Harcourt, 2017).

10. Watson, Renee. Piecing Me Together.
    (Bloomsbury Publishing, 2018).

11. Wilson, Jamia (Author) and Pippins Andrea (Illustrator).

12. Young, Gifted and Black: Meet 52 Black Heroes from Past and Present.
    (Wide Eyed Editions, 2018).

13. Young, Brigit. The Prettiest.
    (Macmillan Publishing, 2020).

Older Books:

1. Abner, Allison and Villarosa, Linda. Finding Our Way: The Teen Girls' Survival
   Guide. (HarperCollins, 1995).

2. Angelou, Maya. Phenomenal Woman.
    (Random House, Inc. 1994). And anything else by Maya Angelou!

3. Banks, Tyra. Tyra's Beauty: Inside & Out.
    (HarperCollins, 1998).

4. Bingham, Mindy, Edmondson, Judy and Stryker, Sandy. Choices: A Teen Woman's
    Journal for Self-Awareness and Personal Planning.
    (Advocacy Press, 1985-Updated 1993).

5. Carroll, Rebecca. Sugar in the Raw: Voices of Young Black Girls in America.
    (Crown Publishers, 1997).

6. Carlip, Hilary. Girl Power: Young Women Speak Out!
    (Warner Books, 1995).

7. Cobain, Bev, R.N.C. (Author) and Verdick, Elizabeth (Editor). When Nothing
    Matters Anymore: A Survival Guide for Depressed Teens.
    (Free Spirit Publishing, Inc., 1998 & 2007).

8. Coles, Joan M. and Post, Elizabeth L. Emily Post's Teen Etiquette.
    (HarperCollins, 1995).

9. Covey, Sean. The 7 Habits of Highly Effective Teens: The Ultimate Teenage Success
    Guide. (Fireside, 1998).

10. Ferebee, Janice. Got It Goin' On: An Image Awareness Guide for Young Ladies.
    (Ferebee Enterprises International, 1996).

11. Ferrell, Pamela. Kids Talk Hair: An Instruction Book for Grown-Ups & Kids.
    (Cornrows & Co., 1999).

12. Hansberry, Lorraine. To Be Young Gifted and Black.
    (Random House, 1998).

13. Hurston, Zora Neale. Their Eyes Were Watching God.
    (Harper Collins, 1998).

14. Johnston, Andrea. Girls Speak Out: Finding Your True Self.
    (Scholastic Press, 1997).

15. Morrison, Toni. The Bluest Eye.
    (Random House, 1993).

16. Petry, Ann. The Street.
    (Houghton Mifflin, 1998).

17. Shange, Ntozake. For Colored Girls Who Have Considered Suicide When the
    Rainbow is Enuf.
    (Simon & Schuster, Inc., 1989).

REFERENCES/RESOURCES

1. www.crisishotline.org (832-416-1177)

2. www.girlshealth.gov

3. Bates, Karen Grisby and Hudso, Karen Elyse. Basic Black: Home Training for Modern Times.(Doubleday, 1996).

4. Broussard, Cheryl D. Sister CEO: The Black Woman's Guide to Starting Your Own Business.(Penguin Group, 1997).

5. Center for Research on Girls & Women in Sport-University of Minnesota. The President's Council on Physical Fitness and Sports Report: Physical Activity & Sport in the Lives of Girls. (Supported by The Center for Mental Health Services/ Substance Abuse and Mental Health Services Administration U.S. Dept. of Health and Human Services).

6. Cole, Harriette. How to Be: Contemporary Etiquette for African Americans. (Simon & Schuster, 1999).

7. Coles, Joan M. and Post, Elizabeth L. Emily Post's Teen Etiquette. (HarperCollins, 1995).

8. Comer, James P., M.D. and Poussaint, Alvin F., M.D. Raising Black Children: Two Leading Psychiatrists Confront the Educational, Social and Emotional Problems Facing Black Children. (Penguin Group, 1992).

9. Duckworth, Angela. Grit: The Power of Passion and Perseverance. (Simon & Schuster, 2018).

10. Ferebee, Janice. Got It Goin' On: An Image Awareness Guide for Young Ladies. (Ferebee Enterprises International, 1996).

11. Foster, Brooke Lea. How To Be Cool. (Washingtonian Magazine, March 2000. Pg. 59).

12. Gandy, Debrena Jackson. Sacred Pampering Principles: An African-American Woman's Guide to Self-Care and Inner Renewal. (William Morrow & Co., 1997).

13. Hersch, Patricia. A Tribe Apart: A Journey Into the Heart of American Adolescence. (Ballantine Publishing Group, 1998).

14. Jakes, T.D. The LADY, Her LOVER, and Her LORD. (G. P. Putnam's Sons, 1998).

15. Kunjufu, Jawanza. Restoring the Village, Values and Commitment: Solutions for the Black Family.
(African American Images, 1996).

16. Meeker, Margart J., M.D. Restoring the Teenage Soul: Nurturing Sound Hearts and Minds in a Confused Culture.
(McKinley & Mann, 1999).

17. Melpomene Institute. Be a Bodywise Woman: Girls, Physical Activity SelfEsteem.
(Melpomene Institute, 1996).

18. Mitchell, Henry H. & Thomas, Emil M. Preaching for Black Self-Esteem.
(Abindon Press, 1994).

19. Pipher, Mary, Ph.D. Reviving Ophelia: Saving the Selves of Adolescent Girls.
(Ballantine Books, 1994).

20. Post, Elizabeth L. Emily Post on Etiquette.
(HarperCollins, 1995).

21. Rutter, Virginia Beane. Celebrating Girls: Nurturing and Empowering Our Daughters.
(Conari Press, 1996).

22. Williams, Terrie. The Personal Touch: What You Really Need to Succeed in Today's Fast-Paced World.
(Warner Books, 1994).

ABOUT THE AUTHOR

(GIGO Alumnae with author: Left to Right – Jessica Artis, Ebony Jackson Griffin, Janice Ferebee & Chavery McCnahan)

Janice Ferebee, MSW, a native New Yorker now living in Washington, DC, is an internationally recognized speaker, author, global female empowerment expert, and DC elected official with a Master of Social Work from the University of Pennsylvania's School of Social Policy & Practice (SP2). She is the founder & Chief Woman Warrior (CWW) of Ferebee Enterprises International, LLC, a global female empowerment social enterprise. With over 40 years' expertise, Janice, the first African American Models Editor for *Seventeen Magazine*, has the proud distinction of being featured on *The Oprah Winfrey Show* and recognized with the 2003 ESSENCE Award for her award-winning *GOT IT GOIN' ON®* *(GIGO)* empowerment brand and program for Black girls and other girls of color. She is a two-time Stage 2B fallopian tube cancer survivor blessed with 30+ years in long-term recovery from drug and alcohol abuse. She has turned her unique personal and professional life experiences into tools to help educators, parents, practitioners, and leaders of girl-serving organizations to empower Black girls and other girls of color to build confidence and cultural pride and develop personal action plans for their lives.

She is a former docent at the historic Smithsonian National Museum of African American History & Culture (NMAAHC) and proud member of Alpha Kappa Alpha Sorority, Inc. (AKA)-- following in the footsteps of her mother, Elizabeth Grant Ferebee, a community activist and special education professional, and descendant of Dr. Dorothy Boulding Ferebee, trailblazing Black female physician, public health pioneer, civil rights and social justice activist, international humanitarian, 2nd National President of the National Council of Negro Women (NCNW), 4th National Vice President of the Girl Scouts of the USA, and 10th International President of AKA Sorority - featured in the NMAAHC.

"Janice addresses today's social issues facing Black women & girls with integrity, humanity, humor (when appropriate), and passion. Her lived experiences make her more than a valuable "go-to" expert. She is a LIVING TESTIMONY!"

\- Overheard at a Presentation

www.janiceferebee.com